feed your family
more from less

Lorna Cooper

SEVEN DIALS

Hi folks,

When I started my Facebook page seven years ago I wanted to help people save money by shopping smartly and cooking creatively. Over the years I have developed my own skills by researching online, experimenting in the kitchen and listening to everyone from top chefs and food-waste champions, to grandmas who lived through rationing. I have watched documentaries about food waste mountains, then switched channels to hear all about food poverty. I have had messages from people who are worried they can't afford to feed their family at all, never mind provide healthy meals on a tight budget. And I have also had messages from people who have never learnt to cook – so for them, it is about gaining the confidence to simply try.

In my first two books I provided meal plans, shopping lists and all the recipes to make eight weeks' worth of meals for £20 a week. I believe those will give the reader a firm foundation on which to build their own meal plans, gain confidence in the kitchen and experiment. This book is slightly different. It will still save you time and money, but it will also teach you how to stretch ingredients; meaning that you can buy more expensive items and know that they will provide more than one meal. The recipes will help you take one key ingredient and make four meals from it. So, for example, you can enjoy a family roast dinner on a Sunday or a fancy meal on a special occasion, which will go on to make three more meals for the week ahead. Or you can freeze them to eat at a later date so you don't have to worry about repetitiveness, and you can switch things up!

This sort of creative cooking was standard years ago when every bit of a single ingredient was used to make various dinners for the family. Back then this was due to cost and food availability, but over the years, with a wider range of food more readily available, we as a nation have lost that skillset. I want to change that. My main goal with this book, is to show that less is definitely more!

xx Lorna xx

CONTENTS

INTRODUCTION

MEAT & FISH

Meat and fish are usually the most expensive elements of people's shopping, so learning how to make the most of them and use up every little scrap can be a huge money saver. If you have read my other books you will know that I bulk out my meals with grains, pulses and vegetables to stretch meat as far as possible. You wouldn't believe the number of times people say to me, 'We only get one meal from a chicken. I don't know how you manage to get four meals for four people!' Upon further investigation it usually transpires that they only use the breast meat and throw the rest of the bird away! My mindset is that if you are going to do that you might as well just cook a couple of chicken breasts.

I slow-cook chicken as it means the meat becomes so tender that it falls off the bone. Then I use the breast meat for a roast dinner for four, filling up the rest of the plate with potatoes, veg, stuffing and Yorkshire puddings. I then allow the chicken to cool (I usually have to hide it in the microwave or else my cat has a good old feast), then I strip the carcass down and put the meat in a bowl and set it aside. I put the bones and skin in a pot which I fill with water, toss in any veg peelings saved from making dinner and a couple of bay leaves or herbs, and then I put this on the stove (or back in the slow cooker) to make a lovely stock. After simmering I take care to strain the stock from the bones, which I pick over again, and any more meat I find I put into the stock to make a delicious soup with the addition of some grains or carbohydrates and some veg.

I shred the meat that I set aside as it makes it stretch further than simply chopping it up. Then I use this meat for two other dishes. People often say, 'That's not enough meat for my family' but I have never had any complaints of anyone being hungry after eating one of my meals! People across this country and beyond eat way more meat than they need to. Some dishes only need a little meat and traditionally only ever had small amounts in them. Let's take as an example a carbonara; one or two slices of leftover gammon from your Sunday joint diced up really small is plenty to put in this pasta dish – there is no need for a full pack of bacon!

In the seven years I've been running my Facebook page, one thing that often comes up is that people just don't know what to do with their leftovers. I think most people will, at some point, find themselves serving up dinner and ending up with a little bit too much of something or other, so the second half of the book looks at what we can do to save this food from being wasted.

PASTA

Let's take a minute to talk about the knack of cooking just enough pasta. HA HA, jokes! No one EVER cooks the correct amount of pasta! Even when following a recipe your typical person will weigh out the pasta, look at it and think, 'Noooo, that's definitely not enough!' And so they add a little more and end up with too much. And it's often too late by the time they realise that their pasta-to-sauce ratio is off and the dish isn't 'saucy' enough. The first tip in this instance is to ALWAYS add your pasta to your sauce rather than pouring the sauce into the pasta. This means you can stop adding pasta before you knock off the ratio.

I know a lot of people don't like reheating pasta, as they feel it just doesn't taste as good or retain its quality, but by adding a few binding ingredients and cooking it in the oven you can make some beautiful meals.

RICE

This is another ingredient that people can find themselves with too much of. And it often ends up in the bin because people are wary of reheating it due to the risks of food poisoning. These risks are very real and occur when rice is kept warm for a while. So if you have leftover rice, you want to cool it down as quickly as possible. You will find out how to do that at the beginning of the rice section (see page 180).

I like to freeze leftover rice as it is so quick and easy to reheat. It means I can have a curry in the slow cooker all day and when I come home I can quickly reheat the rice for a full meal on the table in minutes!

POTATOES

I am going to be completely honest about this – I LOVE potatoes. As a child of the eighties we had potatoes with almost every meal. Pasta and rice were not on the menu at home very often, and never at my nana's house. I went through a phase of not liking meat very much – my aunt said I was just too lazy to chew it (should meat be chewy though?) – so I often ended up with some version of potatoes with cheese melted on top. And if I was to be truthful I would tell you I would quite happily eat that for dinner still!

Because of my insane love of potatoes, it is very rare for me to have leftovers as I just can't resist eating as many as I can, so I started to make extra. Let's be honest here, it is time-consuming to peel and cook potatoes and the starch makes my hands itchy! So if I'm making potatoes for dinner I might as well make a lot and do something fab with the extras. If I know they are for another meal, I manage to NOT eat them all. Mostly! Potatoes are best bought still dirty, in the brown paper sacks.

VEGETABLES

Vegetables are one of the most wasted food items. Once you have served up dinner and only have a spoonful or two left it's easy to think, 'That's not enough to do anything with', so you throw them out or just put extra on the dinner plates, which means they end up in the bin anyway as it's too much.

I'll let you into a little secret here – I don't peel veg unless I absolutely have to! Many of the nutrients in root veg live just under the skin and by peeling them you're usually throwing the goodness away. Also, I come from the school of 'why give yourself extra work?' I just wash my carrots and parsnips and chop them up.

BREAD

OK, more honesty (this is turning into 'confessions of a cookbook author'!), I LOVE bread almost as much as I love potatoes. I try my best to keep on top of the bread usage but I'm not always successful. So sometimes I end up with some slightly stale bread, which isn't the end of the world. I mean, who doesn't love toasted cheese? Right?

Crusty bread is a particular favourite of mine, although unfortunately it doesn't keep very well. But did you know that if you splash it with a little water and pop it in the oven for a few minutes you can revive it? It does need to be eaten immediately afterwards though.

CUPBOARD ESSENTIALS

I often talk about a well-stocked store cupboard in my books and on my Facebook page. I have built mine up over a few years and am now in the position of only needing to restock when I see things on offer, or buy in bulk. But if you are just starting out, I would say you need:

- Tinned tomatoes
- Flour
- Stock cubes
- Lentils
- Oats
- Beans – butter beans, mixed beans, kidney beans or black beans
- Honey
- Lemon juice
- Sugar
- Bread
- Potatoes
- Onions (not by the potatoes as they can cause them to sprout)

HERBS, SPICES & SAUCES

You can easily change up most meals by adding some herbs, spices or sauces. But it can be expensive to buy a cupboard-full in one go! I suggest starting off with some of the most common and gradually building up your supplies. Buy in bulk if you can. Asian supermarkets, wholesalers, eBay and Amazon all sell spices in bulk. If you have a large supermarket nearby they often have a world food aisle where you can buy spices in fairly big bags. Compare the price per kilogram to the little jars a couple of aisles over and you will be astounded!

If you have a fairly well-stocked spice collection, don't buy spice mixes – google what is in them and make your own.

Grow your own herbs, if you can. They don't take up much space and are easy to look after. If you have bought cut herbs and have some left, you can freeze them in oil or butter in ice-cube trays to add to dishes. Or add a sprig or two to a bottle of olive oil and make your own flavoured oil. This is so easy to do and will save you a small fortune!

There are some sauces that I always have in the cupboard for flavouring dishes or dipping. I have found over the years that many own-brand sauces are very cheap and unintentionally lower in salt and sugar than the 'diet' versions of branded items.

If you are just starting your collection, I would advise you buy these items:
- Paprika
- Cinnamon
- Chilli powder
- Garlic
- Ginger
- Curry powder (as mild or as hot as you like)
- Thyme
- Rosemary
- Parsley
- Marjoram
- Chives
- Worcestershire sauce
- Hot sauce
- Mayo
- Sweet chilli sauce

COLD ESSENTIALS

Of course, it's not just cupboard essentials that help with creating meals. Here is a list of what I think you should have in the fridge or freezer to make throwing a meal together easier:

- Milk
- Eggs
- Cheese
- Frozen mixed veg
- Frozen sweetcorn

Finally, just a few words on how this book works. In each meat chapter you will find an initial recipe for the main hero ingredient. Following that will be three soup recipes, plus six other main meal recipes for a family of four. For each meat, you choose one soup and two other mains – this gives you multiple options for what to do with the remaining hero ingredient.

The fish and vegetable sections also give you a main show-stopping meal and three further recipes, again for a family of four.

The next section is called 'Love Your Leftovers' because I want to show you how to reduce your food waste, save money and create beautiful meals or sides from all those little bits you would previously have thrown away. By using all of the food we purchase we not only save money, but can help to save the planet too!

And, like in my two previous books, I have included a basics section, with some recipes that everyone should have at their fingertips.

I hope this all means you can afford to invest in some special ingredients, maybe something you don't usually buy, because you know you can use it to make minimum three further meals!

 I've included some add-ons throughout the book for if you feel like adding something extra special to your meal.

CHICKEN

When I buy a chicken I already know that it is going to make me four meals for four of us. This means that I never put the chicken on the table and let everyone help themselves! I usually cook a whole chicken in the slow cooker, as the meat just slides off the bones and you seem to get so much more meat from it. As we don't eat the skin it doesn't matter to me that it doesn't colour, but you can finish it off in the oven if you want a crispy skin.

For the roast dinner I take off one breast and one thigh. I slice the breast and shred the thigh meat and divide this between the four plates. Served with lots of honeyed veg, mashed potatoes and some stuffing balls, there is plenty of food to fill everyone up.

Once the chicken has cooled, I strip off all the meat and halve it. I usually try to get a mix of white and brown meat in each portion. Next I put everything that is left into a pot or the slow cooker along with any veg peelings (not including potato peelings – they are too starchy and will make your stock gloopy) and a bay leaf, cover it in water and cook for a couple of hours in the pot or overnight in the slow cooker. When that is done the liquid becomes a beautiful stock for making soup and you can usually get a few more pieces of meat to add to it as well.

If I know what recipes I am going to make, and time allows, I will often cook them to either freeze or put in the fridge for during the week. If I haven't decided yet or I don't have time, I will just wrap the chicken well and either freeze it or put it in the fridge. The same goes for the stock, which can be strained and frozen. If you store the chicken in the fridge you have to be aware that it will only keep for three days, so if you store it for two days then make soup on the third day you'll have to eat it all that day or freeze it.

SOUP DISHES

Lemon chicken & pasta soup 18

Roast chicken & vegetable soup 19

Chicken & cauliflower Soup 20

OTHER MEALS

Fakeaway Chicken Quesadilla 23

Chicken Mornay bake 24

Chicken Bolognese 27

Creamy chicken risotto 28

Chicken & bacon salad 29

Chicken & spinach crepes 30

SLOW-COOKED CHICKEN

This is my favourite way to cook chicken. The meat is so tender
and juicy and it just falls off the bones.

....

Serves 4

1 onion, quartered

500g potatoes, peeled
and chopped

2 tsp salt

1 tsp black pepper

1 lemon, zested and
quartered

1 whole chicken

4 tbsp butter

1 garlic clove, minced

2 tsp dried rosemary

2 tsp dried thyme

Put the onion and potatoes in the bottom of the slow
cooker and season with the salt and pepper.

Place the lemon quarters in the chicken's cavity and sit the
chicken on top of the potatoes.

In a small bowl, mix the butter, garlic, rosemary, thyme
and lemon zest. Use your hands to coat the chicken in the
butter mixture. Cook the chicken in the slow cooker on
low for 6 hours or high for 4 hours.

Preheat the oven to 200°C/Fan 180°C/Gas 6.

Take the chicken out of the slow cooker and place on a
baking tray. Lift out the potatoes and place around the
chicken. Roast in the oven for 10 minutes or until the skin
is brown and crispy.

STUFFING BALLS

My kids love these more than anything else on their plate! They fight over them
so I have to make sure not to make an odd number!

....

2 slices of bread

4 sausages, squeezed out
  of their skins

1 tsp dried sage

1 onion, diced

1 egg, beaten

Preheat the oven to 200°C/Fan 180°C/Gas 6.

Lightly toast the bread and either grate or blitz it in a food
processor to make breadcrumbs. Put the breadcrumbs
in a bowl and add the sausage meat, sage and onion.
Get your hands into the bowl and squeeze and mix it
all together. Add the beaten egg and get your hands in
again. Divide the mixture into 8 pieces and roll into balls.

Put the balls on a baking tray and cook for 30 minutes
until golden and cooked through.

HONEY & GINGER-GLAZED ROOT VEG

Something a little bit special to do with root veg, this is worth the extra effort.
Great for special occasions.

....

2 tbsp butter

1 tsp oil

¼ tsp each of salt and black pepper

2.5cm piece of ginger, grated

4 tbsp honey

4 carrots, sliced into strips

2 parsnips, sliced into strips

1 small swede, peeled and sliced into strips

2 tsp dried parsley

Preheat the oven to 200°C/Fan 180°C/Gas 6.

Melt the butter in a bowl in the microwave, then stir in the oil, salt and pepper.

Add the ginger to the honey in another bowl.

Parboil the root veg in a pan of water over a high heat for 5 minutes until just cooked. Drain and tip into a baking tray. Pour the butter mix over the veg and toss around to coat, then drizzle over half the honey and ginger. Put in the oven and roast for 15 minutes. Take out halfway through and toss around to get the glaze on everything.

Remove from the oven at the end of the cooking time, add the remaining honey and ginger mix and stir well to coat.

Sprinkle over the parsley before serving.

LEMON CHICKEN & PASTA SOUP

I realise that this may sound like an odd combination for a soup, but honestly, it's a revelation. You can thank me later!

Serves 8

2 litres chicken stock with cooked chicken pieces

Juice of 2 lemons

1 bay leaf

2 carrots, diced

1 leek, sliced

1 red pepper, deseeded and sliced

200g broken spaghetti or small pasta shapes

200g soft cheese

250g grated cheese

100g kale, chopped

60g parsley, chopped

Salt and black pepper, to taste

Put the chicken stock, lemon juice and bay leaf in a large pan over a medium heat and bring to the boil. Add the carrots, leek and pepper and simmer for about 10 minutes until tender.

Add the pasta to the pan and cook for another 5 minutes or until tender.

Remove the bay leaf. Add the soft cheese, half the grated cheese and the kale and stir through until the cheese has melted and the kale has wilted.

Stir in the parsley. Season with salt and pepper. Serve in individual bowls sprinkled with the remaining grated cheese.

ROAST CHICKEN & VEGETABLE SOUP

This is one of those soups that makes you feel better. Whether you are down in the dumps or feeling ill, a bowl of this will instantly do its job. My kids still ask for some if they have a cold or flu.

Serves 8

1 tbsp oil

2 carrots, peeled and diced

1 parsnip, peeled and diced

1 onion, diced

1 sweet potato, peeled and diced

½ butternut squash, peeled and diced

2 garlic cloves, minced

2 litres chicken stock with leftover cooked chicken pieces

½ tsp dried parsley

½ tsp dried thyme

½ tsp dried rosemary

¼ tsp dried oregano

100g spinach or kale

Salt and pepper, to taste

Preheat the oven to 200°C/Fan 180°C/Gas 6.

Put the oil in a baking tray and toss the carrots, parsnip, onion, sweet potato, butternut squash and garlic until coated. Cook in the oven for 20 minutes, stirring halfway through.

About 5 minutes before the veg is finished cooking, bring the stock to the boil in a large pan. Put half of the veg into the stock and either mash with a potato masher or blend with a stick blender.

Add the rest of the veg and the herbs and bring back to the boil. Taste and add salt and pepper, if needed.

Add the spinach or kale and cook for a couple of minutes until wilted. Serve immediately.

CHICKEN & CAULIFLOWER SOUP

There is only one word for this soup – scrumptious! I can't talk it up enough.

Serves 8

2 tbsp oil

1 onion, diced

5 garlic cloves, grated

5cm piece of ginger, grated

1 small broccoli

1 small cauliflower

¾ tsp red pepper flakes

2 carrots, sliced

2 celery sticks, sliced

2 litres chicken stock with cooked chicken pieces

Salt and black pepper, to taste

Parsley, to garnish

Heat the oil in a large pan over a medium heat. Add the onion, garlic and ginger and cook for 3–4 minutes.

Cut the broccoli and cauliflower into florets, then put in a food processor and blitz to rice-like grains. Add to the pan and cook for 5 minutes or until starting to colour.

Add all the other ingredients and bring to the boil. Simmer for 15 minutes or until the vegetables are soft.

Season with salt and pepper and serve in individual bowls, garnished with parsley.

Pictured opposite: Chicken & cauliflower soup and Roast chicken & vegetable soup

FAKEAWAY CHICKEN QUESADILLA

Save yourself some money by making these at home. They are delicious and taste just like the real thing.

....

Serves 4

8 tortillas

Spray cooking oil

200g grated cheese

200g cooked chicken, shredded

FOR THE SAUCE

3 tbsp mayonnaise

¾ tsp sugar

½ tsp ground cumin

½ tsp paprika

$1/8$ tsp cayenne pepper

$1/8$ tsp garlic powder

2 tsp jalapeños from a jar, minced

Place a large frying pan that has a lid over a very low heat.

In a small bowl, whisk together the ingredients for the sauce. Divide the sauce into 4 and spread over 4 tortillas.

Working with 1 tortilla at a time, spray the pan with a very small amount of cooking oil.

Place the prepared tortilla in the pan and top with about 40g of cheese, 50g of chicken and then sprinkle over a little more cheese. Top with a second tortilla. Cover and let it cook for about 2 minutes or until the shell begins to turn golden brown.

Flip over the quesadilla, cover the pan with the lid and cook for another 2 minutes. Repeat with the other prepared tortillas.

Slice with a pizza cutter and enjoy.

CHICKEN MORNAY BAKE

I love chicken and I love leeks, so you can imagine how much I enjoy this recipe!
Luckily, I am not the only one. My family like it too.

....

Serves 4

60g butter

1 onion, finely diced

1 leek, halved lengthways
and finely sliced

¼ tsp curry powder

50g plain flour

500ml milk

200g cooked chicken,
shredded

1 x 340g tin sweetcorn

1 red pepper, deseeded
and sliced

100ml double cream

100g grated cheese

Salt and black pepper, to
taste

Preheat the oven to 180°C/Fan 160°C/Gas 4.

Melt the butter in a large pan and add the onion, leek and
curry powder and cook for 2–4 minutes.

Add the flour and stir continuously for 2 minutes. Pour
in the milk and stir until the sauce comes to the boil.
Reduce the heat and continue stirring until the sauce
thickens. Season to taste. Add the rest of the ingredients
except the grated cheese.

Grease a large casserole dish and pour in the chicken mix.
Sprinkle over the cheese and bake for 25–30 minutes.

CHICKEN BOLOGNESE

Something a little bit different. Who said Bolognese can only
be made with beef mince? Not me!

....

Serves 4

1 tbsp oil

1 large onion, diced

3 garlic cloves, grated

1 red pepper, deseeded
and chopped

100g mushrooms, sliced

2 tbsp tomato puree

1 tsp dried oregano

1 chicken stock cube

2 x 400g tins chopped
tomatoes

200g cooked chicken,
shredded

300g spaghetti

Handful of basil leaves, to
serve

¼ tsp chilli flakes, to serve

Heat the oil in a large pan over a low heat and fry the
onion for 5 minutes until softened. Add the garlic and
pepper and cook for 2–3 minutes more – be careful not
to burn the garlic.

Add the mushrooms, tomato puree and oregano, then
crumble over the stock cube and stir thoroughly. Add the
tinned tomatoes and chicken, stir, and increase the heat.
Bring to the boil then reduce the heat and gently simmer
for 20 minutes.

Meanwhile, cook the spaghetti in a large pan of salted
boiling water according to the packet instructions.

Serve the chicken Bolognese on top of the spaghetti,
with the basil and chilli flakes scattered over.

CREAMY CHICKEN RISOTTO

Everyone loves risotto, don't they? Even my fussiest kids can't get enough of this recipe.

....

Serves 4

2 tbsp butter

225g Arborio rice

1 leek, finely sliced

2 garlic cloves, minced

750ml chicken stock

200g cooked chicken, shredded

2 tbsp cream cheese

1 tsp chopped chives

50g Parmesan cheese, grated

Salt and black pepper, to taste

Melt the butter in a large frying pan over a medium heat. Add the rice, leek and garlic and stir thoroughly until coated in the butter. Add a ladle full of stock and stir until it is absorbed then add another ladle and repeat until it is all absorbed. Stir through the cooked chicken and the cream cheese and continue to stir to evenly distribute. Taste and season.

Stir again and sprinkle with the chives and Parmesan. Ensure the chicken is piping hot before serving.

CHICKEN & BACON SALAD

My daughter loves this recipe. As does her best friend . . . I first made this when they were teenagers and it became a weekly dinner for them before they headed out to Explorers on a Wednesday night! There is a recipe to make your own salad cream in the basics section.

....

Serves 4

2 little gem lettuces, sliced

6 radishes, sliced thinly

6 spring onions, sliced thinly

½ cucumber, halved lengthways then sliced

8 cherry tomatoes, cut in half

200g cooked chicken, shredded

150g bacon, cooked and diced

100ml salad cream

Put all the salad ingredients into a large serving bowl. Add the chicken and bacon and stir well.

At the very last moment, just before serving, stir in the salad cream.

CHICKEN & SPINACH CREPES

This recipe involves a little bit of work, but I promise it is worth it.
Your family will appreciate the effort.

....

Serves 4

FOR THE CREPE BATTER

2 eggs

120g plain flour

125ml milk

125ml water

A pinch of salt

1 tbsp vegetable oil

FOR THE FILLING

200ml single cream

100g soft cheese

3 garlic cloves, grated

½ tsp dried marjoram

1 tbsp vegetable oil

200g cooked chicken, shredded

200g spinach

50g grated cheese

Salt and black pepper, to taste

First make the crepe batter. Beat the eggs in a mixing bowl with a whisk, then add the flour, milk, water and salt and whisk until smooth and lump free. Rest the batter for 20 minutes before cooking.

Preheat the oven to 180°C/Fan 160°C/Gas 4.

While the batter rests, make the filling. Combine the cream, soft cheese, garlic and marjoram in a bowl and add to the oil in a frying pan over a medium–high heat. Stir in the chicken and spinach. Cook for about 5 minutes until the chicken is hot, the spinach has wilted and the sauce has thickened. Season to taste.

Lightly grease a medium frying pan and put it over a medium heat. Add a ladleful of batter and swirl to spread out and cover the base of the pan. Cook for 3–4 minutes until golden, then flip and repeat. Stack the cooked crepes on a plate while you cook the rest.

Place a heaped tablespoon of filling in the centre of a crepe and roll it up. Repeat to use all the crepes and filling. Place the filled crepes in a casserole dish and sprinkle the grated cheese over. Bake in the oven for 10 minutes until the cheese is golden and bubbling.

BEEF

When I 'invest' in a piece of beef I always do so knowing that it isn't just for one meal. I usually aim for a 1.4kg piece of meat that I can get for around £9–10. The first thing I do is cut off 200g to use for soup. I then usually cook the rest of the beef joint, although occasionally, depending on what other meals I want to use it for, I will cut off another piece or two first.

Cooking the whole joint of meat at once means that the 'extra' meals can be made much quicker, which is handy for midweek dinners. Once it is cooked I cut it in half, giving me 600g to slice and serve with all the usual lovely trimmings. The other 600g I cut in half again. These two pieces will be used in two more recipes. If I am not making these within a couple of days, I wrap the meat well and freeze it. But if time allows I will often cook the extra recipes at the same time and either freeze them or put them in the fridge to eat during the week.

Eating this way doesn't have to mean you only have one type of meat for the whole week. By freezing the meals, or just the meat, you can use the beef over the whole month.

HERO DIE

Yorkshire pudding

Crushed mashed potatoes

SOUP DISHES

Jamaican beef soup 38

Beef noodle soup 39

Beef & tomato soup 40

OTHER MEALS

Beef & barley paella 42

Beef cobbler 45

New York-style beef sandwich 46

Roast beef Thai red curry 49

Roast beef fritters 50

Roast beef hash 53

ROAST BEEF

If you are going to buy a nice bit of beef, you need to make sure you do it justice. After lots of trial and error over the years, this is how I make mine and I guarantee it is amazing.

....

Serves 4

1.2kg beef joint

2 onions, quartered

1 garlic bulb, cut in half

1 tbsp mustard

¼ tsp each of salt and
   black pepper

Take the joint out of the fridge half an hour before you want to put it in the oven, to bring to room temperature.

Preheat the oven to 180°C/Fan 160°C/Gas 4.

Put the onions and garlic in the base of a roasting tin. Season the mustard with the salt and pepper and mix to combine. Pat the beef joint dry with kitchen paper, then smear it all over with the mustard. If you have a rack for your roasting tin, sit the beef on it. If not, just sit the joint on top of the onions and garlic.

Place the beef in the oven to roast to your preferred doneness. For rare beef you want to cook it for 20 minutes per 500g plus 20 minutes, so for this size it is 1 hour 8 minutes; for medium beef, 25 minutes per 500g plus 20 minutes, so 1 hour and 19 minutes; while for well done it is 30 minutes per 500g plus 20 minutes, so 1 hour and 32 minutes.

At the end of the cooking time, remove the joint from the oven, wrap it in foil and allow to rest for 20 minutes.

Once rested, cut in half and use one half for the roast dinner, then cut the other section in half again, individually wrap each piece and store them in the fridge or freezer.

YORKSHIRE PUDDINGS

The number of people over the years who have said they cannot make Yorkshire puddings astounds me. I urge you to give this recipe a try and see how you get on. You can make this batter in advance and chill in the fridge.

....

3 eggs

120g plain flour

500ml milk

¼ tsp each of salt and black pepper

2 tbsp oil

Preheat the oven to 200°C/Fan 180°C/Gas 6. Put an empty Yorkshire pudding tin in the oven for 10 minutes until it is hot.

Beat the eggs in a large mixing bowl. Add the flour, milk and seasoning and mix until you see bubbles – using an electric whisk or even a blender makes this much easier.

Put a little oil in 8 holes of the pudding tin and put it back in the oven until it is smoking.

Give the batter a last stir, then pour it into the same 8 holes – it should start to cook and sizzle straight away. Place the tin on the top shelf of the oven. After 10 minutes, open the oven door for a couple of seconds and let some of the steam out. Close the door and cook for a further 10–15 minutes until they are golden and well risen.

You can also use this recipe to make 2 large Yorkshire puddings.

CRISPY ROAST POTATOES

Everyone loves roast potatoes, don't they? Especially when they are light and fluffy inside and crispy on the outside. Try this recipe and you'll never use another one again.

....

1kg potatoes, peeled

2 tbsp oil

2 tbsp flour or semolina

½ tsp each of salt and black pepper

Preheat the oven to 200°C/Fan 180°C/Gas 6.

Boil the potatoes in a large pan of water until almost cooked – should take approximately 15 minutes.

Put the oil in a large roasting tray and place in the oven for at least 15 minutes to heat up.

Mix the flour or semolina and salt and pepper together in a mixing bowl. Drain the potatoes in a colander, sprinkle over the flour mix and bash them around in the colander so they get a little roughed up and coated in the flour. Transfer to the tray and stir carefully – that oil is HOT! Try to make sure they all get some oil on them. Put them back in the oven on the top shelf and cook for 30 minutes.

Take them out every 10 minutes and move them around to ensure they are coated with oil and crisping evenly. Once golden brown and crispy, remove and serve.

JAMAICAN BEEF SOUP

This soup is so full of flavours that combine nicely to give you a warming and spiced soup – but not too spicy to put people off.

Serves 8

30ml oil

1 large onion, diced

4 spring onions, sliced

1 red pepper, deseeded and sliced

2 garlic cloves, grated

2.5cm piece of ginger, grated

1 tbsp dried thyme

2 tsp allspice

1 tsp smoked paprika

2 bay leaves

1 tsp hot sauce

3 tbsp tomato puree

2 litres beef stock

200g roast beef, cut into small chunks

4 carrots, cut into large chunks

500g potatoes, peeled and cut into large chunks

Heat the oil in a large pan over a medium heat. Add the onion, spring onions, pepper, garlic, ginger, thyme, allspice, paprika, bay leaves and hot sauce to the pan. Cook, stirring, for about 2–3 minutes until the onions are translucent.

Add the tomato puree. Stir for another minute, then add the stock to the pan and bring to a boil. Throw in the beef, carrots and potatoes. Reduce the heat, cover and simmer gently until the potatoes and carrots are soft – usually for around 30 minutes.

Remove the bay leaves and serve.

feelin' fancy?

Serve with fresh, buttered crusty bread.

BEEF NOODLE SOUP

I'm sure you have all tried chicken noodle soup at one point in your life. I love it,
so I thought, why not make a beef version? I am happy to announce it is just
as good and is now a regular make in my house.

Serves 8

2 medium onions, cut into small wedges

2 celery sticks, chopped

200g mushrooms, sliced

3–4 garlic cloves, grated

2 tbsp butter

200g roast beef, cut into small chunks

2 litres beef stock

1 tbsp Worcestershire sauce

300g uncooked egg noodles

Salt and black pepper, to taste

In a large pot, cook the onions, celery, mushrooms and garlic in the butter until the vegetables have softened and the onions are golden.

Stir in the beef. Pour in the beef stock and the Worcestershire sauce, stirring to mix, and season to taste with salt and pepper (how much you add will depend on how seasoned the beef and broth already are, so be careful here). Bring to the boil, then stir in the egg noodles. Reduce the heat to a simmer and cook, stirring occasionally, for 10–12 minutes or until the noodles are tender.

Serve hot.

BEEF & TOMATO SOUP

I have called this a soup but it really could be called a stew, as once the bread soaks up the stock it is so thick. I love it so much and it is very filling.

Sewrves 8

30ml oil

1 onion, chopped

2 carrots, sliced into half rounds

4 garlic cloves, minced

½ tsp dried rosemary

¼ tsp each of salt and black pepper

750ml tomato juice

500ml beef stock

200g roast beef, thinly sliced

300g day-old baguette, French stick or ciabatta bread, torn into large cubes

50g Parmesan cheese, grated

A few leaves of basil or parsley, torn

Heat the oil over a medium–high heat in a large saucepan. Cook the onion, carrots, garlic, rosemary and salt and pepper, stirring occasionally, until softened, about 8 minutes.

Pour in the tomato juice and beef stock and bring to the boil. Reduce the heat and simmer for 10 minutes.

Add the beef and bread, stirring until the bread has 'melted' into the liquid and the soup thickens, about 8 minutes.

Serve in individual bowls and divide the cheese and herbs between them, sprinkling them over the top.

Pictured opposite: Jamaican beef soup and Beef & tomato soup

BEEF & BARLEY PAELLA

Have you ever tried paella without rice before? This one uses pearl barley instead and works really well! It is a big favourite in my house.

....

Serves 4

1 tbsp oil

300g roast beef, diced

1 tbsp smoked paprika

4 celery sticks, sliced

1 red pepper, deseeded and sliced

1 green pepper, deseeded and sliced

100g pearl barley

1 garlic clove, sliced

6 sprigs of thyme

1 tsp saffron

500ml beef stock

100g kale or spinach, torn or shredded

Place a 30cm paella pan, frying pan or cast-iron casserole dish over a high heat and heat the oil. Add the beef and sprinkle over the paprika.

Add the celery and peppers, pearl barley, garlic, thyme, saffron and stock and bring to the boil. Reduce the heat to low, cover and simmer for 45 minutes or until the beef and pearl barley are tender. If the liquid reduces too much, add a little water to keep the beef moist.

Add the shredded kale or spinach in the last 2 minutes of cooking to heat through.

BEEF COBBLER

I love a good beef stew. It is like a hug in a bowl. And the addition of the savoury biscuits takes it to a whole other level.

....

Serves 4

FOR THE STEW

2 tbsp oil

1 large onion, diced

1 litre beef stock

300g roast beef, diced

6 medium carrots, cut into large chunks

1 small swede, cut into large chunks

3 parsnips, cut into large chunks

500g baby potatoes, sliced in half

1/2 tsp black pepper

1 bay leaf

Salt and black pepper, to taste

2 tbsp cornflour

1 tbsp chopped parsley (optional)

FOR THE BISCUITS

300g self-raising flour

70g grated Cheddar cheese

225ml double cream

Preheat the oven to 180°C/Fan 160°C/Gas 4.

Add the oil to a large ovenproof dish with a lid, over a medium heat. Fry the onion until soft, about 5 minutes.

Pour in the stock. Add the beef along with the veg, pepper and bay leaf and bring to the boil. Cover the pan with the lid and transfer to the oven. Cook until the veg and potatoes are tender to the bite, about 45 minutes.

Meanwhile, prepare the biscuits. Use a rubber spatula to combine the flour, cheese and cream in a mixing bowl just to a workable dough. Turn the dough out onto the work surface (lightly dusted with flour) and use a bench scraper or knife to fold the dough over itself 3–4 times.

Shape the dough into a mound and use your hands to gently pat it to about 2.5cm thick. Use a biscuit cutter to cut out rounds. Gather the leftover dough and repeat cutting out and reshaping until you have used it all. Chill the biscuits until ready to bake.

Once the stew is cooked, taste for salt and pepper, then remove the bay leaf. Remove from the oven and raise the oven temperature to 220°C/Fan 200°C/Gas 7.

Whisk the cornflour with 3 tablespoons of cool water and stir this into the stew to thicken the liquid. Stir in the parsley, if using. Arrange the biscuits over the top of the stew, return to the oven with the lid off, and bake until the biscuits are golden brown, about 15 minutes.

NEW YORK-STYLE BEEF SANDWICH

No need to fly off to America for this speciality when you can recreate it at home.
Try to get the beef sliced as thinly as possible for the best results.

....

Serves 4

60g plain yoghurt

30g mayonnaise

50g crumbled strong
cheese

2 tbsp chopped chives or
spring onions

Spray cooking oil

4 small plum tomatoes,
halved lengthways

1 small red onion,
quartered

300g roast beef, sliced
really thin

4 lettuce leaves

4 sandwich buns, toasted

In a small bowl, combine the yoghurt, mayonnaise, cheese
and chives or spring onions.

Coat a large non-stick frying pan with oil spray. Set over a
medium–high heat until hot. Place the tomatoes and onion
in the pan. Cook for 2–3 minutes on each side, or until
lightly charred.

Layer the roast beef, onion, tomatoes and lettuce on
the bottoms of the buns. Drizzle with the yoghurt and
mayonnaise dressing. Cover with the bun tops.

Serve with corn cobbettes and sweet potato
wedges.

ROAST BEEF
THAI RED CURRY

If you have kids who are veg refusers, you can easily mash down the butternut
squash into the curry sauce and they won't know! Either way it is a
lovely dish – not too spicy, but still with a kick.

....

Serves 4

1 tbsp oil

1 medium onion, finely
  diced

1 tbsp grated ginger

4 garlic cloves, grated

200ml beef stock

4 tbsp red Thai curry
  paste

300g roast beef, cut into
  cubes

1 medium butternut
  squash, peeled,
  deseeded and diced

1 x 400ml tin coconut milk

2 tbsp lime juice

Salt, to taste

Heat the oil in a large pan over a medium heat. Add the
onion, ginger and garlic and cook until they are soft, about
5 minutes.

Stir in the beef stock and curry paste. Add the beef to the
pan and bring to the boil. Reduce the heat, cover the pan
and simmer gently for 20 minutes.

Add the squash to the pan and continue to cook for
15 minutes, or until the squash is tender.

Pour in the coconut milk and lime juice and season to
taste with salt.

ROAST BEEF FRITTERS

Yeah, really! I know they sound strange but do give them a go.
The kids will love them.

....

Serves 4

70g plain flour

70g self-raising flour

1 tsp salt

1 egg, beaten

250ml milk

1 tsp black pepper

250g roast beef, diced

1 tbsp butter

Sift the flours and salt into a large mixing bowl, then stir in the egg, milk and pepper. Stir to form a smooth, pancake-like batter, then add the beef to the batter and mix in well.

Heat a frying pan and add the tablespoon of butter. Once the butter has melted, add spoonfuls of the batter to the frying pan and cook until golden brown on both sides.

Serve with chips and beans for dinner or with tomato or BBQ sauce for lunch.

ROAST BEEF HASH

I love a hash. They are so easy to make and so easy to adapt to your taste.
The sweet potato in this one switches it up a lot.

....

Serves 4

3 large sweet potatoes,
  peeled and chopped
  into chunks

1 large onion, diced

1 red pepper, deseeded
  and sliced

3 garlic cloves, grated

2 tbsp oil

300g roast beef, shredded

2 tbsp Worcestershire
  sauce

100ml apple cider vinegar

4 eggs

Salt and black pepper, to
  taste

Place the sweet potatoes in a medium-sized pan and
cover with water. Boil for 3–5 minutes, until the potatoes
are just softened. Drain and cool slightly, then dice the
potatoes into small cubes.

In a large frying pan, fry the onion, pepper and garlic in
the oil until the onion is translucent, about 5 minutes. Add
the cooked sweet potatoes and fry for 2–3 minutes. Stir
in the beef and Worcestershire sauce and cook for 3–4
minutes, stirring occasionally. Season to taste, if needed.
Stir in the vinegar and cook for 2 minutes longer.

Make 4 wells in the hash and crack 1 egg into each.
Season with salt and pepper, then cover the pot and leave
on the heat until the eggs are cooked to your liking – do
not stir.

Serve immediately.

PORK

When choosing a joint of pork to cook I usually go for a leg joint if I am making a roast dinner. Shoulder joints need to cook longer and slower, so they are perfect in the slow cooker or in a casserole dish on low in the oven. I love to make a pot roast with my shoulder joint. As it is a one-pot meal it means we can enjoy a tasty, filling, roast-style dish but I don't have to be in the kitchen for hours. I can prep in the morning and go off out or spend time with the family and let it cook slowly to perfection!

Again, I try to go for a 2kg piece of meat, which should cost about £8. Try to get a piece with a nice fatty layer, as even if you aren't going to use it for crackling it keeps the meat nice and juicy as it cooks.

With this one I don't tend to cut off the meat for my soup, as boiling pork doesn't give much of a stock, so it's a waste of time and energy. I cook the whole joint and then cut it up for my recipes. I use about 800g for my roast dinner, then set aside the rest for the soups and further recipes. If you are not cooking the extra meals straightaway, you need to wrap the pork very well before either putting it in the fridge (for up to 3 days) or freezing it (for up to 3 months) as it can dry up and be quite tough.

HERO DISH

Slow-... ...oast ...

SOUP DISHES

Mexican pork soup 58

Pork & bean soup 61

Pork & cauliflower soup 62

OTHER MEALS

Pork chop suey 64

Congee pork 67

Pork jambalaya 68

Pulled pork nachos 71

Sheet-pan Cuban sandwiches 72

Southwestern pork lettuce wraps 75

SLOW-ROAST PORK

This is my favourite way to cook pork. I can prep and put it in the slow cooker, go out and enjoy my day and come home to a stunning dinner!

....

Serves 4

4 carrots, thickly sliced

4 parsnips, thickly sliced

2 onions, quartered

750g new potatoes, larger ones halved

2 garlic cloves, minced

2 tsp paprika

2 tsp onion powder

2 tsp garlic powder

1 tsp chilli powder

½ tbsp salt

½ tsp black pepper

2kg pork shoulder

2 tbsp oil

1 tbsp balsamic vinegar

2 tbsp cornflour

Put all the prepped vegetables and potatoes in the bottom of the slow cooker. Add the garlic and stir through.

Mix the dried spices and salt and pepper together. Pat dry the pork shoulder with some kitchen paper and rub the spices into the meat.Heat the oil in a large frying pan until hot. Pour in the balsamic vinegar and stir quickly, then add the pork shoulder. Cook for 3 minutes then turn the meat over and cook for another 3 minutes.

Transfer the pork to the slow cooker, on top of the veg. Cover and cook on high for 4 hours or low for 8 hours.

Remove the meat and vegetables from the slow cooker. Wrap the meat in foil and leave to rest. Transfer the veg to a tray or serving plate and keep warm in a low oven.

Mix the cornflour with a little cold water to make a thick paste, then stir it into the juices in the slow cooker. Turn the cooker up to high and put the lid back on. Leave for 10 minutes then check to see if it has thickened enough. You may need to add a little more cornflour if it hasn't.

Cut off 800g of pork, shred and serve with the roasted veg, potatoes and gravy. Store the rest safely, ready for the extra meals.

MEXICAN PORK SOUP

Another soup that is a little bit different to what you are used to, but it works!
And it is very tasty . . .

Serves 4

½ tbsp oil

1 onion, diced

1 garlic clove, minced

1 tsp ground cumin

1 tsp ground coriander

1 tsp smoked paprika

½ tsp mild chilli powder

1 x 400g tin chopped
   tomatoes

800ml vegetable stock

200g cooked pork, diced

1 x 400g tin kidney beans,
   drained

150g frozen veg

½ red pepper, deseeded
   and chopped

Heat the oil in a large pan and cook the onion for 2–3
minutes until soft. Add the garlic and the spices and cook
for a further 1 minute, stirring constantly.

Add the chopped tomatoes and stock. Bring to the boil
and simmer for 5 minutes. Use a stick blender to blitz the
soup to make it smooth.

Add the pork, kidney beans, frozen vegetables and red
pepper and simmer for 5 minutes.

*Serve with some grated cheese and tortilla
chips for dipping.*

feelin'
fancy?

PORK & BEAN SOUP

If you are looking for a really filling soup, then you will love this one.
Packed with everything you need to satisfy hungry tummies!

Serves 4

200g broth mix

2 tsp oil

1 onion, diced

1 celery stick, sliced

1 carrot, peeled and sliced

2 garlic cloves, minced

1 x 400g tin chopped
tomatoes

500ml vegetable stock

2 tsp dried mixed herbs

Salt and black pepper, to
taste

100g cooked pork,
shredded

1 x 400g tin mixed beans,
drained

Soak the broth mix overnight in 1 litre of cold water. Drain and rinse once ready to use.

Heat the oil in a large pan over a medium heat and fry the onion, celery, carrot and garlic until soft. Add the broth mixture and fry for 2–3 minutes more.

Add the tomatoes, stock and herbs and season to taste. Stir in the pork and mixed beans. Simmer for 30 minutes, adding more water if the mixture gets too thick.

PORK & CAULIFLOWER SOUP

This is such a delicious creamy soup that it is a firm favourite of mine. And my eldest son, who doesn't like cauliflower, ate it for years without realising what was in it, before he caught me making it one day!

Serves 4

200g cooked pork, shredded

1 large potato, peeled and cut into chunks

1 medium cauliflower

1 celery stick, sliced

1 medium carrot, peeled and sliced

1 onion, diced

½ tsp dried thyme

500ml chicken stock

¼ tsp paprika

⅛ tsp each salt and black pepper

500ml milk

Add all the ingredients, except the milk, to a large pan and bring to the boil over a high heat. Reduce the heat to medium, cover and simmer for 20 minutes.

Remove the cauliflower with a slotted spoon, transfer it to a blender with the milk and blitz to blend.

Pour the cauliflower milk mix back into the soup, heat through briefly, and enjoy.

PORK CHOP SUEY

A fab quick and easy stir-fry. I love the crunch from the beansprouts!

....

Serves 4

1 tbsp oil

½ onion, sliced

1 garlic clove, minced

2.5cm piece of ginger, grated

200g beansprouts

300g stir-fry veg mix

200g cooked pork, diced

100ml vegetable stock

1 tsp dark soy sauce

1 tsp cornflour

2 spring onions, sliced

Salt and black pepper, to taste

Cooked noodles, to serve

Heat the oil in a wok over a high heat. Fry the onion, garlic and ginger for 1 minute.

Add the beansprouts and stir-fry veg and fry for 30 seconds. Then add the pork and fry for a further 30 seconds.

Pour in the vegetable stock and leave for 1 minute or until it starts to boil. Add the soy sauce and stir well, then season with salt and pepper to taste. Mix the cornflour with a little cold water to blend, then stir into the sauce and cook until the sauce has thickened.

Mix through the spring onions and serve with freshly cooked noodles.

CONGEE PORK

This is such a filling and tasty dish I don't know why I had never had it until I was in my thirties.

....

Serves 4

800g cooked rice

1.2 litres chicken stock

2 eggs, beaten

2 tbsp oil

2 tsp red pepper flakes or
  cayenne pepper

200g cooked pork,
  shredded

6 spring onions, sliced

Chopped coriander, to
  garnish

Put the rice and stock into a large pan and cover with a lid. Bring to the boil then simmer, uncovered, over a low heat for 20 minutes.

Stir in the beaten eggs and cook for 2 minutes more.

Meanwhile, mix the oil with the pepper flakes or cayenne in a small bowl.

Divide the congee among 4 serving bowls, then top each bowl with some pork, the spring onions and the seasoned oil. Serve garnished with a little chopped coriander.

PORK JAMBALAYA

As well as using up cooked pork5 you can also use leftover rice for this dish.
It is one of John's favourite dishes yet he still can't say it properly. Silly man!

....

Serves 4

1 tbsp oil

1 onion, diced

2 celery sticks, sliced

2 garlic cloves, minced

2 tsp paprika

½ tsp cayenne pepper

3 tbsp tomato puree

300g cooked pork, diced

2 red peppers, deseeded
  and sliced

150ml vegetable stock

500g cooked rice

Heat the oil in a large wok or frying pan. Add the onion and celery and cook for 5 minutes, then stir in the garlic, paprika, cayenne and tomato puree and cook for 1 minute, stirring continuously.

Add the pork, peppers, stock and cooked rice and cook for a further 2 minutes until most of the stock has been absorbed.

Remove from the heat and serve.

PULLED PORK NACHOS

With BBQ sauce and cheese, you just know this is one of Kyle's favourites. You can tell because he starts lurking around the kitchen when he knows I'm making it for dinner!

....

Serves 4

250g cooked pork, shredded

200ml BBQ sauce

400g tortilla chips

2 jalapeño peppers, sliced and deseeded

200g grated cheese

4 spring onions, diced

200g salsa, to serve

200ml soured cream, to serve

Preheat the oven to 180°C/Fan 160°C/Gas 4.

Mix the pork with one-third of the BBQ sauce.

Line a baking tray with enough tortilla chips to cover the bottom and up the sides. Add a layer of pulled pork, jalapeños, BBQ sauce and cheese. Top with the remaining chips, the remaining pulled pork, jalapeños and BBQ sauce. Then top with the remaining cheese.

Bake in the oven for 10–15 minutes or until the cheese is melted. Remove from the oven and top with the spring onions.

Serve with salsa and soured cream.

SHEET-PAN CUBAN SANDWICHES

Another something a bit different. It's well worth the extra
effort to make, in my opinion.

....

Serves 4

3 garlic cloves, minced

½ tbsp salt

2 tsp ground cumin

1 tsp black pepper

1 tsp dried oregano

100ml fresh orange juice

4 tbsp lime juice

3 tbsp olive oil

300g cooked pork, sliced
thinly

90g butter, softened

2 small baguettes, halved
lengthways

25g mustard

300g cooked ham, sliced

200g dill pickles, sliced

200g Swiss cheese, sliced

In the bowl of a food processor, combine the garlic, salt, cumin, pepper, oregano, orange juice, lime juice and olive oil and process until the garlic is fully minced. Transfer to a large sealable container, add the cooked pork to the marinade and put in the fridge for at least 1 hour.

Heat the oven to 200°C/Fan 180°C/Gas 6.

Butter the outsides of the bread and lay the bottom halves on a baking sheet. Spread the bread halves with a thin layer of mustard, then top with the sliced ham and marinated pork. Add some pickles and Swiss cheese, then put the bread lids on the sandwiches.

Put a second baking sheet on top and press down firmly, then sit something oven-safe and heavy on top. Put in the oven for about 20 minutes until the cheese has melted.

Cut into portions and serve.

 feelin' fancy?

Serve with salad and potato wedges.

SOUTHWESTERN PORK LETTUCE WRAPS

These are my go-to if we are eating in the garden. They are so summery and tasty, but also filling.

....
Serves 4

170ml mayonnaise

80ml buttermilk

4g coriander, chopped

1 red pepper, deseeded and sliced

1 tbsp garlic powder

$1/3$ tbsp onion powder

$1/3$ tbsp dried oregano

$1/8$ tsp ground pepper

$1/3$ tsp paprika

2 tbsp lime juice

1 tsp granulated sugar

1 tsp salt

¾ tsp ground cumin

1 x 400g tin black beans, drained

250g cooked rice

2 spring onions, sliced

1 tbsp oil

8 lettuce leaves

300g cooked pork, shredded

60g salsa

100g grated cheese

Process the mayonnaise, buttermilk, coriander, red pepper, garlic and onion powders, oregano, pepper, paprika, lime juice, sugar, ½ teaspoon of the salt and ½ teaspoon of the cumin in a food processor or blender until smooth, about 1 minute. Cover and chill until ready to use.

Stir together the beans, rice, spring onions and one-third of the mayonnaise mixture. Cover and chill until ready to use.

Spoon one-eighth of the bean mixture onto each lettuce leaf, and top each with some of the shredded pork, 1 teaspoon of salsa and some cheese. Serve with the remaining mayonnaise mixture alongside.

GAMMON

I used to always buy a 2kg gammon joint to make my four meals from, but recently it's become cheaper to buy two 1kg joints from my local supermarket. And I don't mean just a little bit cheaper! A 2kg joint costs £10 but a 1kg joint is only £3.40, meaning for 2kg it's £6.80. The lesson here is to ALWAYS check the price per kilogram of food. Never ASSUME that the bigger size is better value!

So I buy two 1kg joints but cook them together. I start the cooking process for my gammon by boiling it. This means I can then use the cooking water as stock for soup. Once my gammon is cooked, I remove it from the pot. I cut off 800g for my roast. I usually coat this and finish it off in the oven, then serve it with roast potatoes and cauliflower, broccoli and leek in a cheese sauce.

The leftover 200g gets shredded and used with the stock to make my soup and the other 1kg gets cut in half for the two extra recipes. Or occasionally for even more than two. Gammon is such a flavourful ingredient that you don't need a lot to get a good taste of it. I will say this, though: if I am not using it up pretty quickly, I have to freeze mine because I can't help myself and pop a bit in my mouth every time I open the fridge.

HERO DISH

SOUP DISHES

Lentil soup with crispy leek croutons 82

Ham & potato soup 83

Creamy yellow split pea soup 84

OTHER MEALS

Ham & pea salad 86

Ham & leek pie 89

Ham cobbler 90

Ham, Brie & cranberry pasta 93

Cheese & ham soufflé 94

Ham roly poly 97

GAMMON JOINT

Gammon is my favourite roast meat. I honestly love it so much. I have to be so strict with myself as I could easily just keep eating it and eating it and eating it!

....

2kg gammon joint or 2 ×
  1kg gammon joints

2 litres water

1 tsp peppercorns

1 celery stick, roughly
  sliced

2 small carrots, topped,
  tailed and quartered

1 onion, quartered

FOR THE GLAZE

2 tbsp brown sugar

4 tbsp light soy sauce

4 tbsp marmalade

Put the gammon joint(s) in a large pan and add the water, peppercorns, celery, carrots and onion. Bring to the boil, reduce the heat, then cover and simmer for 60 minutes for 2 × 1kg joints or 1 hour 40 minutes for a 2kg joint.

Remove the gammon from the pan, but remember to save the water – you can strain this stock through a sieve to remove any bits, then use it in soup.

Preheat the oven to 200°C/Fan 180°C/Gas 6.

Cut 800g of meat off the joint and place this portion in a baking tin. Slice the remaining gammon into the weight you need for any other recipes, wrap, and store in the fridge for 3 days or freezer for 3 months.

In a small bowl, mix the brown sugar with a little hot water until dissolved. Add the soy sauce and marmalade and stir well. Spread this mix over the gammon joint and cook in the oven for 10 minutes. Turn the gammon, spoon the glaze that's in the bottom of the tin over the meat and cook for another 10 minutes.

Remove from the oven and leave to rest for 10 minutes before slicing and serving. Use the glaze in the tin to drizzle over the gammon on the serving plate.

CAULIFLOWER, BROCCOLI & LEEK IN CHEESE SAUCE

I have always loved cauliflower cheese, so when someone told me they made cheesy leeks, I was intrigued. I tried them and was equally impressed. This version came about because I had some broccoli left over and thought I'd just add it too. Good call – it's delicious!

....

1 small cauliflower, broken into florets

1 small broccoli, broken into florets

2 leeks, cut in half lengthways and sliced

FOR THE CHEESE SAUCE

25g butter

25g plain flour

500ml milk

200g grated cheese

Put the cauliflower, broccoli and leeks in a large pan and cover with water. Bring to the boil over a high heat, then reduce the heat and simmer for 20 minutes.

Meanwhile, make the cheese sauce. Melt the butter in a medium pan, then stir in the flour and mix to a thick, smooth paste. Gradually add the milk while continuing to stir. Bring to the boil, then reduce the heat and simmer gently until the sauce is thick and glossy. Stir in three-quarters of the cheese.

Drain the veg and add to a casserole dish or small baking tray. Pour over the sauce, then top with the remaining cheese. Pop it in the oven for 15 minutes when you take the gammon out to rest.

CRISPY, SPICED SWEET POTATOES

These potatoes complement the other dishes so well and make a nice change from the traditional roast potatoes.

....

4 sweet potatoes

4 tbsp butter

1 tsp garlic powder

1 tsp ground cumin

1 tsp paprika

1 tsp chilli flakes

Preheat the oven to 200°C/Fan 180°C/Gas 6.

Wash the potatoes and prick all over with a fork or sharp knife, then microwave on high for 4 minutes.

Melt the butter in the microwave and brush some of it onto 4 metal skewers. Insert the skewers lengthways into the potatoes. With a sharp knife, cut down to the skewer every centimetre along each potato (or every few millimetres if you want thinner slices). Put the potatoes on a baking tray and brush with the remaining butter.

Combine all the dry ingredients and sprinkle this mix over the potatoes. Cook in the oven for 40 minutes, turning them halfway through the cooking.

LENTIL SOUP WITH CRISPY LEEK CROUTONS

I love lentil soup, and so do my kids. I wanted to see if I could take it up a level, though, so I played around adding spices and came up with this version – which was very well received when I served it up as a midweek dinner with crusty bread!

Serves 8

2 tbsp oil

1 onion, diced

2 carrots, diced

1 celery stick, sliced

2 garlic cloves, minced

½ tsp turmeric

½ tsp ground ginger

1 tsp ground cumin

½ tsp dried chilli flakes

½ tsp sea salt

1 x 400g tin chopped tomatoes

1.5 litres ham stock

200g red lentils

2 tbsp butter

2 leeks, cut in half lengthways and chopped

200g cooked ham, shredded

Heat the oil in a large pan and cook the onion, carrots and celery for 5 minutes. Add the garlic, turmeric, ginger, cumin, chilli flakes and salt and cook for another 2 minutes.

Add the tomatoes and stock, then tip in the lentils, bring to the boil and simmer for 20 minutes until the lentils have softened.

Meanwhile, heat the butter in a separate pan and fry the leeks for 10–15 minutes until they go nice and crispy.

Blitz the soup with a hand blender until smooth, then ladle into individual bowls. Top each with some of the crispy leek croutons and the shredded ham.

HAM & POTATO SOUP

This hearty, filling soup has to be served with crusty bread smothered
in thick butter . . . it's practically the law. Enjoy!

Serves 8

1 tbsp oil

1 onion, diced

3 carrots, diced

3 celery sticks, diced

4 potatoes, peeled and
diced

3 garlic cloves, minced

200g cooked ham,
shredded

1 litre ham stock

2 bay leaves

1 tsp dried thyme

Salt and black pepper, to
taste

Heat the oil in a large pan and fry the onion, carrots and
celery for 5 minutes.

Add the potatoes, garlic and ham and cook for 2–3
minutes. Pour in the stock, then add the bay leaves, thyme
and seasoning. Bring to the boil, then reduce the heat and
simmer for 20 minutes or until the potatoes are tender.

Remove the bay leaves. Take out half the volume of
the soup with a ladle into a bowl and blitz with a hand
blender, or transfer to a blender. Return this blended soup
to the remaining soup in the pan and stir thoroughly to
combine. Heat through before serving, if necessary.

CREAMY YELLOW SPLIT PEA SOUP

This is basically a pea and ham soup, but the addition of a few ingredients takes it to a whole different level. You have to try this one to believe it!

Serves 4

1 tbsp oil

1 onion, diced

2 garlic cloves, minced

2.5cm piece of ginger, grated

250g yellow split peas

1 litre ham stock

¾ tsp turmeric

½ tsp black pepper

100ml coconut milk

200g cooked ham, shredded

A few coriander leaves, to garnish

Heat the oil in a large pan over a medium heat and cook the onion for 3–4 minutes. Add the garlic and ginger and cook for 2–3 minutes. Add the split peas, stock, turmeric and black pepper. Bring to a gentle boil, reduce the heat and simmer for 45 minutes. Keep an eye on the liquid levels – if it is drying out, add a little water.

Remove from the heat and blitz with a hand blender until smooth. Stir through three-quarters of the coconut milk, then stir in the cooked ham.

Divide among 4 bowls and serve with a swirl of coconut milk and sprinkle of coriander.

feelin' fancy? This is really nice served with warm garlic flatbreads!

Pictured opposite: Lentil soup with crispy leek croutons and Creamy yellow split pea soup

HAM & PEA SALAD

It may sound like all these different ingredients shouldn't be in the same dish,
but when you have made it once you will make it all the time.

....

Serves 4

500g frozen peas,
    defrosted

2 celery sticks, sliced

4 spring onions, chopped

4 radishes, sliced

100g dry roasted peanuts

½ avocado, peeled, pitted
    and diced

1 tbsp white wine vinegar

1 tsp Dijon mustard

¼ tsp sugar

2 tbsp olive oil

85g watercress, torn

500g cooked ham,
    shredded

Defrost the peas by placing in a colander and holding under a running cold tap. Put the drained peas, celery, spring onions, radishes, peanuts and avocado in a large bowl.

Whisk the white wine vinegar, mustard and sugar together in a bowl and gradually stir in the olive oil. Toss the salad with the dressing.

Put the watercress in 4 bowls and top with the salad. Scatter the shredded ham on top.

HAM & LEEK PIE

We love a pie in our house – and this is one of the best I've ever made. It has all my favourites in it. If you don't have the time or inclination for the whole recipe, you can buy pastry instead of making your own. I won't tell anyone, I promise!

....

Serves 4

FOR THE PASTRY

400g plain flour, plus extra for dusting

Pinch of salt

200g chilled butter, cubed, plus extra for greasing

3–4 tbsp cold water

FOR THE SAUCE

25g butter

25g plain flour

300ml milk

FOR THE FILLING

2 leeks, cut in half lengthways and sliced

50g butter

2 tbsp mustard

500g cooked ham, shredded

1 egg, beaten

First make the pastry. Mix the flour and salt in a large mixing bowl, then add the butter and, using your fingertips, rub the mix together until it resembles breadcrumbs (or use a food processor if you have one). Add the cold water 1 tablespoon at a time and mix until it comes together as a dough. Wrap well in cling film and place in the fridge for at least 30 minutes.

Meanwhile, make the sauce. Melt the butter in a large pan, then add the flour and whisk for 2–3 minutes. Gradually add the milk, whisking continuously, until you get a smooth sauce. Simmer until the mix has thickened.

Finally, make the filling. Gently fry the leeks in the butter in a frying pan for 5 minutes until softened but not coloured. Tip the leeks into the white sauce. Add the mustard and cooked ham. Set aside to cool.

Preheat the oven to 200°C/Fan 180°C/Gas 6. Grease a medium pie dish, approximately 24 x 18cm.

Split the pastry ball in half and roll out on a lightly floured surface to double the size of your pie dish. Line the dish with half of the pastry. Add the filling into the pastry case, then cover with the other half of the pastry. Pinch around the edges with a fork to seal. Cut a couple of slits in the top of the pastry lid, then brush it with the beaten egg.

Bake in the oven for 10 minutes, then reduce the heat to 180°C/Fan 160°C/Gas 4 for 25–30 minutes.

HAM COBBLER

My kids love this cobbler. I always get a positive reception when I say this is what I am making for dinner. Happy kids = happy mum!

....
Serves 4

2 tbsp oil

400g mushrooms, sliced

2 garlic cloves, minced

2 leeks, sliced

2 carrots, sliced

6 tbsp plain flour

2 tbsp mustard

1 tsp dried thyme

½ tsp each of salt and black pepper

400ml ham stock

2 tsp balsamic vinegar

100ml water

500g cooked ham, cubed

2 tbsp Greek yoghurt

FOR THE COBBLER

120g butter, frozen

350g self-raising flour

¼ tsp paprika

¼ tsp each of salt and black pepper

1 tsp baking powder

50g cheese, grated

120ml buttermilk

Heat the oil in a large frying pan and fry the mushrooms and garlic for 5 minutes. Add the leeks and carrots and stir to combine. Reduce the heat and cook the veg for 5 minutes.

Sprinkle in the flour gradually and stir until combined. Add the mustard, thyme, salt and pepper and give it a stir. Now add the stock, vinegar and water and bring to the boil. Add the ham and simmer for 5 minutes. Take off the heat and allow to cool slightly before stirring in the yoghurt. Taste and add more salt and pepper, if required. Tip the mixture into a casserole dish.

Preheat the oven to 180°C/Fan 160°C/Gas 4.

Grate the frozen butter into a large mixing bowl, then add the flour, salt and pepper and baking powder and mix gently. Add the paprika, salt and the grated cheese, and stir again. Pour in the buttermilk and stir with a metal fork to create a very rough dough. Drop tablespoons of the dough on top of the casserole mix in the dish.

Cook for 30 minutes in the oven, until the dough is risen, cooked and golden.

HAM, BRIE & CRANBERRY PASTA

This recipe was created one Boxing Day when we had all this left over from Christmas Day. My daughter asked if I could make something with the Brie and cranberry sauce, so this dish was born. Now we make sure to have all the ingredients set aside so we can make it again and again!

....

Serves 4

250g Brie

2 garlic cloves, sliced

3 sprigs of thyme, leaves only

500g pasta

3 tbsp Parmesan cheese, grated

2 tbsp butter

500g cooked ham, cubed

50g frozen cranberries or 4 tsp cranberry sauce

Salt and black pepper, to taste

Preheat the oven to 180°C/Fan 160°C/Gas 4.

Slice the top rind off the Brie and lay the garlic slices and thyme leaves on top. Place the Brie on a small baking tray and cook for 20 minutes.

Meanwhile, cook the pasta following the packet instructions. Once the pasta is ready, remove a ladle of the cooking water to a jug and set aside. Drain the pasta then return it to the pan. Mix in 2 tablespoons of the Parmesan, the butter and salt and pepper. Add a few splashes of the reserved water and stir through the pasta. Put the lid on the pan and set aside.

When the Brie is completely melted, scoop it out of the rind and spoon it into the pasta. Add some more of the reserved water if the pasta is too hard to stir, then stir to combine. Stir in the ham, and if you are using frozen cranberries, stir them in now. Pour the pasta mix into a buttered baking dish and sprinkle with the remaining Parmesan. If using cranberry sauce, dot it over the top now.

Cook in the oven for 20 minutes.

CHEESE & HAM SOUFFLÉ

There is really only one word to describe this dish – and it is YUM! My mouth
is watering so much just thinking about eating this gorgeous soufflé.

....

Serves 4

120g butter, melted, plus
  extra for greasing

16 slices of bread

400g cooked ham, cubed

400g mature Cheddar
  cheese, grated

400g Swiss cheese,
  grated

6 eggs, beaten

700ml milk

½ tsp onion salt

2 tbsp mustard

1 tsp paprika

150g cornflakes, crushed

Butter a 23 x 33cm casserole dish.

Cut the crusts off the bread, then cut the slices into cubes.
Line the bottom of the dish with half of the bread cubes.
Top with the ham and cheeses. Top with the remaining
bread cubes.

In a bowl, mix the eggs, milk, onion salt, mustard and
paprika. Pour over the bread, cover the dish with cling film
and refrigerate for at least 6 hours.

Preheat the oven to 180°C/Fan 160°C/Gas 4.

Combine the cornflakes and the 120g butter and spread
this mix on top of the bread cubes. Cook for 40–50
minutes until puffed up and golden. Serve immediately.

HAM ROLY POLY

This is a fairly old recipe that your grandma probably made a version of. It can also be made with cooked bacon if you don't have any leftover ham. Look out for 'cooking bacon' in the shops and fry it off with the onion.

···············

Serves 4

1 tbsp butter

1 onion, diced

200g cooked ham, sliced thin and cut into cubes

1 tbsp chopped sage leaves

½ tsp black pepper

FOR THE PASTRY

225g plain flour, plus extra for dusting

100g suet

¼ tsp salt

Heat the butter in a large frying pan and fry the onions until cooked but not coloured. Take off the heat and stir in the cooked ham, sage and pepper.

Put the flour, suet and salt into a large mixing bowl. Add enough cold water to bind, then tip the pastry onto a floured sheet of greaseproof paper and roll into a rectangle approximately 35 x 25cm.

Tip the ham mix evenly across the pastry, leaving a 1cm border around the edge. Roll the pastry as you would a Swiss roll, bringing the short end over the filling and carefully rolling, keeping the filling inside – use the paper to help you. Seal the final edge with water. Loosely wrap the pastry in the greaseproof paper, then transfer to a sheet of foil and loosely wrap it again, tying the ends like a Christmas cracker to secure.

Set it in a steamer basket inside a large pan with a lid and cook for 2½ hours. Alternatively, you can cook it in the oven at 200°C/Fan 180°C/Gas 6. Half fill a deep roasting tin with boiling water and place it in the bottom of the oven, then set the wrapped roly poly on another tray on the shelf above. Cook in the oven for 40 minutes.

LAMB

Let me start this off by saying, yes, lamb is expensive. I don't usually buy it unless it's either on offer or reduced, then I freeze it until I have a special occasion on which to use it. I prefer lamb shoulder when I do buy it and I try to get at least a 1.5kg joint. That said, I wouldn't walk past a lamb leg in the yellow-sticker section! Just remember, if you do have a leg bone you can boil it for stock for soup.

I like to slow-roast a lamb shoulder and serve it with smashed sweet potatoes, hasselback potatoes and steamed asparagus served inside a large Yorkshire pudding. The addition of the Yorkshire pudding means I can get away with not serving as much meat, as visually it reduces the size of the plate and physically helps to fill tummies, too. When I have cooked my lamb joint I cut off 200g for soup and set it aside. I then cut the remaining joint roughly in half and slice one half for the roast dinner. Then I cut the other piece in half for the two other meals. As with the other meats, if you're not using the lamb straightaway, wrap it well and freeze, or put it in the fridge to eat within a week.

HERO DISH

Roast lamb shoulder 100

Hasselback potatoes 102

SOUP DISHES

Lamb & pepper soup 103

Lamb shawarma soup 105

Lamb Scotch broth 106

OTHER MEALS

Lamb biryani 108

Spicy lamb tagine 111

Shepherd's pie 112

Meatloaf 115

Ragu 116

Lamb pitas 118

ROAST LAMB SHOULDER

I used to be scared to cook lamb. It was a fairly expensive joint to buy and I was
worried about not doing it justice. No need for you to feel the same way, as
this recipe is easy to follow and gives fab results!

....

Serves 4

1.5kg lamb shoulder joint

1 bunch of rosemary
  sprigs

1 bulb of garlic, left whole
  and unpeeled

1 tbsp oil

¼ tsp each of salt and
  black pepper

Preheat the oven to 220°C/Fan 200°C/Gas 7.

Using a sharp knife, mark a series of slashes on the meat.
Lay half the rosemary and half the garlic cloves in the
base of a deep roasting tray. Sit the lamb on top. Pour a
little oil over the lamb, sprinkle on the salt and pepper and
rub it into the meat. Put the remaining rosemary and garlic
on top of the lamb. Cover the tin tightly with foil – make
sure there are no gaps.

Turn the oven down to 180°C/Fan 160°C/Gas 4. Put the
lamb in the oven and cook for at least 4 hours.

Take it out of the oven, transfer the lamb to a plate, use
the cooking foil to wrap the joint and set aside to rest for
20 minutes.

Cut 200g of meat off the joint for soup. Cut off 700g to
slice for the roast, then cut the other piece in half, wrap
well and store in the fridge or freezer.

See page 36 for the Yorkshire pudding recipe and serve
these with the lamb.

HASSELBACK POTATOES

A good alternative to traditional roasties, these look fabulous on the table! You can jazz them up with some extra seasonings if you want to play about, but I like to keep them simple.

....

500g baby potatoes

4 tbsp butter, melted

½ tsp each of salt and black pepper

Preheat the oven to 220°C/Fan 200°C/Gas 7.

Put a skewer through a few potatoes – this just gives you a guide so you don't slice right through them. Slice every centimetre along each potato (or every few millimetres if you want thinner slices) on one side down to the skewer, then remove the skewer and place the potato in cold water. Repeat until all the potatoes are cut. Drain them and place cut side up on a baking tray.

Drizzle over half the butter and season with the salt and pepper. Bake for 40 minutes – basting occasionally with the butter. Remove from the oven and drizzle with the remaining butter, then serve.

LAMB & PEPPER SOUP

This soup is so delicious. The addition of the allspice takes it from a normal soup to a top-notch one! You will not be disappointed.

Serves 6

4 tbsp oil

1 red pepper, deseeded and quartered

1 orange pepper, deseeded and quartered

1 green pepper, deseeded and quartered

2 garlic cloves, minced

25g fresh ginger, grated

2 onions, diced

4 tsp allspice

2 celery sticks, sliced

4 carrots, sliced

1 litre lamb stock

200g cooked lamb, diced

Heat the oil in a large pan over a high heat and fry the peppers for 5 minutes. Add the garlic, ginger and onions and cook for 2 minutes. Add the allspice, celery and carrots, pour in the lamb stock and stir everything together. Bring to the boil, then cover with a lid and simmer for 1 hour.

Remove a few peppers and set aside. Roughly blend the soup with a hand blender, then return the peppers to the pan with the lamb and heat through.

LAMB SHAWARMA SOUP

I don't really know how to describe this soup so you will have to try it yourself!
I don't think you will regret it.

....

Serves 6

2 tbsp oil

2 garlic cloves, minced

1 onion, diced

2 tbsp tomato puree

2 tsp ground cumin

2 tsp ground coriander

2 tsp paprika

1 tsp ground cinnamon

½ tsp cayenne pepper

½ tsp black pepper

1 tsp salt

2 carrots, diced

2 x 400g tins chickpeas,
    drained and rinsed

1 x 400g tin chopped
    tomatoes

750ml vegetable stock

200g cooked lamb, diced

300g spinach

Heat the oil in a large pan over a high heat and fry the garlic and onion for 2 minutes. Add the tomato puree and cook for 1 minute, then add the spices, pepper and salt, mix thoroughly and cook for 1 minute. Add the carrots, chickpeas, tomatoes and stock, stir and bring to the boil. Reduce the heat, cover and simmer for 10 minutes.

Add the cooked lamb and stir in the spinach. Once the spinach has wilted, taste and season if needed.

Ladle into bowls.

Pictured opposite: Lamb & pepper soup and Lamb shawarma soup

LAMB SCOTCH BROTH

I love Scotch broth. My nana made us a version with ham bones when I was younger, which was delicious, but this is the more traditional dish – which is also delicious!

Serves 6

30g butter

1 onion, diced

1 leek, sliced

2 carrots, sliced

1 small swede, diced

70g split dried peas

110g barley

2.5 litres lamb stock

¼ white cabbage, shredded

200g kale, shredded

200g cooked lamb, shredded

2 tbsp chopped parsley

Salt and black pepper, to taste

Melt the butter in a very large pan over a medium heat. Add the onion and leek and cook for 5 minutes until softened but not coloured. Add the carrots and swede and stir, then tip in the split peas and barley and pour in the stock. Bring to the boil, then cover and simmer for 1 hour.

Add the shredded cabbage, kale and lamb and cook for another 15 minutes.

Stir through the parsley, taste, then season if required and serve.

LAMB BIRYANI

Looking for something a little bit different to do with cooked lamb?
You have come to the right place.

....

Serves 4

1 tbsp oil

1 onion, finely diced

2 garlic cloves, minced

1 red chilli, chopped

2 tbsp rogan josh curry
paste

300g cooked lamb, diced

250g basmati rice

550ml hot chicken stock

100g kale, roughly
chopped

150g raita or plain
yoghurt

1 lemon, cut into wedges

Heat the oil in a large pan and cook the onion for 5 minutes. Stir in the garlic, chilli and rogan josh paste, then add the cooked lamb and stir well. Stir in the rice and stock and bring to the boil, then cover and cook over a low heat for 10 minutes. Add the kale for the last 4 minutes of the cooking time.

Remove from the heat and leave to sit for 5 minutes.

Put the biryani into 4 bowls and top with some cooling raita or yoghurt. Squeeze a little lemon juice on top and serve.

SPICY LAMB TAGINE

You don't need a tagine to cook this one, as a large pot will do the job.
This will make you dream about exotic holidays in sunny places!

....

Serves 4

1 onion, diced

3 garlic cloves, minced

1 x 400g tin chopped
   tomatoes

2 chillies, chopped

1 tsp chilli powder

1 tsp paprika

1 tsp ground ginger

1 tsp turmeric

1 tsp ground cinnamon

1 tsp salt

10 dried apricots

300g cooked lamb, finely
   diced

1 x 400g tin chickpeas,
   drained and rinsed

Heat the oil in a large pot or tagine and cook the onion over a high heat for 2 minutes. Reduce the heat and add the garlic and cook for 30 seconds. Stir in the tomatoes, spices, salt and apricots and cook for 5 minutes. Add the cooked lamb and chickpeas and stir well. Cover and cook for 25 minutes.

feelin' fancy?   Serve with couscous.

SHEPHERD'S PIE

The ultimate winter comfort food. I could eat this a couple of times a week, no problem. I love mine served with cabbage and peas – my mouth is watering just thinking about it!

....
Serves 4

1 tbsp oil

2 onions, diced

2 carrots, finely diced

2 celery sticks, sliced

2 garlic cloves, minced

1 tbsp finely chopped rosemary

2 tbsp tomato puree

300g cooked lamb, finely diced

500ml lamb stock

1 tbsp Worcestershire sauce

800g potatoes, peeled and cubed

1 tbsp butter

60ml milk

Salt and black pepper, to taste

Preheat the oven to 200°C/Fan 180°C/Gas 6.

Heat the oil in a medium pan over a low heat and gently fry the onions, carrots and celery for about 10 minutes. Add the garlic and rosemary and cook for 1 minute. Add the tomato puree, chopped lamb, stock and Worcestershire sauce and season. Bring to the boil, reduce the heat and simmer for 15 minutes.

Meanwhile, boil the potatoes in a pan of water until soft. Drain well, then add the butter, milk and a little salt and mash until smooth.

Place the lamb mix in the bottom of a baking dish. Spoon over the mashed potato and smooth out, dragging a fork across the mash. Place in the oven and cook for 25 minutes.

MEATLOAF

This has been a favourite with my kids for a long time, and one of the few dishes that would get a YAY from all three when they found out it was for dinner. Ultimate taste test!

....

Serves 4

4 slices of bread

300g cooked lamb, finely diced

1 onion, diced

1 garlic clove, minced

1 apple, quartered and cored

1 tbsp curry paste

1 egg, beaten

½ tsp each of salt and black pepper

1 tbsp oil

Preheat the oven to 180°C/Fan 160°C/Gas 4.

Put the bread in a food processor and blend into coarse breadcrumbs. Tip out the breadcrumbs and add the lamb, onion, garlic, apple quarters and curry paste to the food processor. Blitz for a minute then add the breadcrumbs, egg and salt and pepper. Blitz again just for 30 seconds. If you don't have a food processor, just grate the bread and veg, and dice or shred the lamb, then get your hands in the bowl to mix thoroughly.

Line a 900g loaf tin with baking paper and press the meatloaf into the tin. Cover with foil and cook for 30 minutes. Remove the foil and cook for a further 10 minutes.

Allow to cool in the tin for 10 minutes, then slice and serve.

feelin' fancy?

We love this with mashed potato and mixed veg in winter and sweet potato fries and salad in summer!

RAGU

This is one of my favourite ways to use up cooked lamb. It is quick and simple to do and tastes great. I like to serve it with garlic toast.

....

Serves 4

1 tbsp oil

1 onion, diced

3 garlic cloves, minced

400g pasta

2 tbsp tomato puree

1 tsp dried oregano

1 carton passata

1 tsp brown sugar

1 carrot, grated

50g red lentils

1 tbsp Worcestershire sauce

300g cooked lamb, finely diced

125g ricotta cheese

Heat the oil in a large pan over a low heat and fry the onion for 2 minutes. Add the garlic and cook for 2 minutes more.

Cook the pasta following the packet instructions.

Stir the tomato puree and oregano into the onion and garlic, then add the passata, brown sugar and grated carrot. Tip in the lentils and add 200ml of water. Bring to the boil, then reduce the heat. Add the Worcestershire sauce and diced lamb and cover with the lid. Cook for around 15 minutes until the lentils have softened, stirring occasionally and making sure there is enough liquid. If it starts to stick, add more water.

Serve over the pasta and top with a little ricotta cheese.

LAMB PITAS

A lovely summery dish that tastes like it could have come from the kebab shop,
but it is much better for your waistline – and your bank balance!

....

Serves 4

300g plain yoghurt

1 garlic clove, minced

2 tsp mint sauce

2 little gem lettuces

1 cucumber

4 tomatoes

4 pita bread

300g cooked lamb, sliced
thinly

Salt and black pepper, to
taste

Mix the yoghurt, garlic and mint sauce together in a bowl
to make the dressing, seasoning to taste.

Slice the lettuce, cucumber and tomatoes, tip into the
bowl and toss with the dressing.

Cut the pita breads in half to make a pocket, then heat in
the toaster.

Stuff the pita breads with the dressed lettuce, cucumber,
tomatoes and the lamb slices.

Enjoy!

FISH

Fish is a very important part of our diet. It can be expensive but if you think smartly when you buy it and be creative when you are cooking it, a little can go a long way. I have been lucky enough a few times to find a whole side of salmon in the reduced section of the supermarket, but even at full price if I manage to stretch it to four meals I think it is a smart investment. And it feels like a big luxury!

For a less-expensive option I have included trout. Now, the best way to get hold of some trout is to get friendly with someone who fishes as a pastime. These guys often come home with more fish than they know what to do with, so a cordial 'Hey man, I love trout and would be happy to take some off your hands anytime you have some spare' will usually result in a call every now and then to see if you want any!

Or if you are lucky enough to live near a harbour, pop down and look for a guy in a yellow or orange waterproof jacket and trousers and ask politely if they have any fish for sale.

It is often easier and cheaper to buy fish already frozen and filleted, but fresh whole fish are a treat and of course you can use the head and bones to make a delicious stock.

HERO DISH

Oven-baked salmon 1?3

Creamy spring ... 124

SOUP DISH

Slavic salmon soup 125

OTHER MEALS

Salmon & broccoli risotto 126

Salmon & creamed spinach pasta 129

HERO DISH

Whole ...

SOUP DISH

Smoky trout chowder 132

OTHER MEALS

Trout, goat's cheese & beetroot salad 134

Trout cakes 137

OVEN-BAKED SALMON

Salmon is such a lovely fish and can make a fabulous centrepiece on the dinner table. In this recipe we manage to save half the fish for other recipes whilst still having the option of serving it as a full side. By removing the bones it makes it easier for people to help themselves.

....

Serves 4

2 large potatoes, sliced thinly

2 large carrots, sliced thinly

2 tbsp each of salt and black pepper

2kg whole salmon, scaled, gutted and cleaned

½ bunch of thyme leaves

4 sprigs of rosemary, leaves stripped

1 whole garlic bulb, separated and crushed but skin still on

2 lemons, peeled and roughly chopped

1 tbsp oil

Preheat the oven to 180°C/Fan 160°C/Gas 4.

Lay the sliced potatoes and carrots flat in a large roasting tin and sprinkle over half the salt and pepper.

Place the salmon flat and make 5 slits on the top down to the bone, then turn over and do the same again. Fill the slits with the thyme, rosemary, garlic and lemon pieces. Sit the salmon on top of the potatoes and carrots, brush with the oil, sprinkle over the rest of the salt and pepper and cook in the oven for 40 minutes.

Remove from the oven, cover with foil and leave to rest for 10 minutes. Cut the head and tail off the salmon and set aside. Carefully peel back the skin from one side of the fish. Using a slotted spatula, remove the flesh from the bones in sections. Set aside. Use the spatula to hold the bottom flesh down and then carefully lift up the spine. Put it with the head and tail and save to make stock.

You can now either serve the bottom flesh on the skin as it is for people to help themselves or scrape it off the skin and serve in portions with the potatoes and carrots and crisp spring veg. Divide the meat from the top of the fish into (approximately) 3 x 200g for the soup and extra meals.

CRISPY SPRING VEG

Serves 4

1 tbsp olive oil

2 little gem lettuces, cut into quarters

6 spring onions, sliced

150g radishes, trimmed and halved

50ml water

1 tbsp each of salt and black pepper

200g asparagus, trimmed and cut into thirds

Bunch of parsley, roughly chopped

Heat the oil in a large frying pan over a high heat and cook the lettuce, spring onions, radishes, water and salt and pepper for 5 minutes. Add the asparagus and cook for 2 minutes more.

Remove from the heat and stir in the chopped parsley. Serve with the baked salmon.

SLAVIC SALMON SOUP

This is fast becoming one of my favourite soups, and I believe you will love it too.

Serves 4

1.5 litres water

1 onion, diced

1 carrot, sliced

2 large potatoes, cubed

200g salmon, deskinned and diced into 2.5cm pieces

½ tsp salt

¼ tsp black pepper

½ tsp dill

2 bay leaves

Bring the water to the boil in a pan over a high heat. Add the onion to the water, cover, lower the heat and simmer for 7 minutes. Add the carrot, replace the lid and simmer for another 7 minutes. Add the potatoes, turn the heat back up until boiling, then reduce to a gentle simmer and cook for another 10 minutes.

Add the salmon and salt, pepper, dill and bay leaves, cover and cook for 15 minutes. Check the potatoes and carrots are soft, and if not, cook for another 5 minutes.

Remove the bay leaves, season if necessary, and serve.

SALMON & BROCCOLI RISOTTO

This dish looks and tastes amazing. It is so flavourful and tasty that no one would ever imagine it costs so little and is so easy to make.

....

Serves 4

500g broccoli florets, stems removed and diced

60ml butter

1 tbsp olive oil

1 onion, finely diced

250g Arborio rice

125ml white wine

900ml vegetable stock

1 tbsp each of salt and black pepper

50g Grana Padano cheese, grated

200g cooked salmon, flaked

Bring some salted water to the boil in a large pan. Add the broccoli florets and cook for 3 minutes. Drain and run under cold water until cool, then set aside.

In another pan, melt the butter and oil over a medium heat and cook the onions and broccoli stems for 3 minutes until softened. Tip in the rice and stir well until the rice is coated in the butter and oil mixture. Pour in the wine and cook until it has evaporated. Add 125ml or around half a cup of hot vegetable stock and continue stirring until it is absorbed. Repeat until you have just 250ml of stock left.

Add the broccoli florets and the rest of the stock and stir just to reheat, then add the salt and pepper and the cheese at the last minute and stir through.

Divide the risotto among 4 deep bowls and top with the salmon flakes.

SALMON & CREAMED SPINACH PASTA

Another gorgeous recipe that looks and tastes indulgent. But it really isn't! You can suitably impress your family and friends with this luscious dish.

....

Serves 4

350g spaghetti

¼ tsp dill

4 garlic cloves, minced

200g baby spinach

200g frozen peas

8 tbsp lemon juice

2 tbsp cream cheese

½ tsp black pepper

200g cooked salmon, flaked

Cook the spaghetti following the packet instructions. Drain, but reserve 1 ladleful of the cooking water.

Put the pan back on a low heat and add the spaghetti, dill, garlic, spinach and peas. Stir through and cook until the spinach has wilted. Add the cream cheese, pepper and pasta water and stir through until the cheese has melted.

Divide among 4 bowls and put the flaked salmon on top.

feelin' fancy?

Serve with a crisp side salad.

WHOLE COOKED TROUT

If you are lucky enough to know a fisherman you can put this showstopper on the table for little to no cost, but even if you don't you can still do it relatively cheaply. And by removing half the fish before serving you can guarantee that it will do another three meals!

....

Serves 4

2 tbsp oil

6 tomatoes, sliced

1 red onion, finely sliced

30g dill, roughly torn

30g parsley, roughly torn

2kg whole trout

1 tbsp salt

3 tbsp black pepper

1 lemon, sliced

200g cherry tomatoes, sliced

50g butter, melted

Preheat the oven to 180°C/Fan 160°C/Gas 4.

Pour half of the oil into a large baking tray and add one-third of the tomatoes, onion, dill and parsley. Sit the trout on top and season with the salt and 1 tablespoon of the pepper.

Put another third of the tomatoes, onions, dill and parsley in the cavity along with the lemon, then top with the remaining vegetables and herbs. Scatter the cherry tomatoes around.

Mix the remaining oil with the melted butter and remaining pepper. Drizzle this over the fish and cook for 25 minutes.

To serve, remove the head just behind the gills – put it aside to make stock. Slice open the skin along the stomach, across the tail and along the back, using your knife to get between the skin and the meat. Put the skin with the head, then remove the meat down to the bones. Carefully remove the bones and add to the head and skin. Section this into 2 x 200g and 1 x 300g portions for your soup and extra meals. Wrap this and store in the fridge or freezer.

Serve the bottom half of the fish as it is for people to help themselves, or scrape from the skin with a spoon and portion up. Serve with the roasted tomatoes.

feelin' fancy?

Also serve with steamed asparagus and lemon rice or couscous.

SMOKY TROUT CHOWDER

I love a good chowder, and this is a really good chowder! It is smoky and spiced just enough to give a little heat, but the inclusion of the cream means it isn't too spicy.

....

Serves 4

1 tbsp butter

2 carrots, sliced

1 onion, finely diced

1 tbsp oil

2 large potatoes, cut into chunks

2 parsnips, cut into chunks

1 tbsp paprika

½ tsp cayenne pepper

1 tsp each of salt and black pepper

750ml fish stock

200ml water

150ml single cream

1 bay leaf

200g cooked trout, flaked

Coriander leaves, to garnish

Melt the butter in a large pan over a medium heat and cook the carrots and onion for 5 minutes. Add the oil, stir, then add the potatoes and parsnips and cook for 10 minutes. Add the spices, salt and pepper and cook for another 2 minutes. Pour in the fish stock and water and bring to the boil.

Remove a ladleful of the hot stock and mix with the single cream (this will stop it curdling when you add it to the pan). Pour this cream mix into the pan, reduce the heat, add the bay leaf and stir well. Cover and cook for 20 minutes.

Remove the bay leaf, mash down lightly with a fork and add the trout. Heat through for a couple of minutes and then serve with a little torn coriander on top.

TROUT, GOAT'S CHEESE & BEETROOT SALAD

I may have got a bit carried away with this one. This is my go-to when I am trying to impress; lovely, quick and easy to put together, it looks and tastes very posh!

....

Serves 4

4 tbsp olive oil

4 tbsp balsamic vinegar

Juice of 1 lemon

2 tsp mustard

¼ tsp each of salt and black pepper

200g salad leaves

200g cooked beetroot, cut into chunks

60g goat's cheese, crumbled

200g cooked trout, flaked

60g walnuts, chopped

Mix the oil, vinegar, lemon juice, mustard and salt and pepper in a bowl.

Add the salad leaves and mix through the dressing. Divide the salad among 4 bowls and top with the beetroot, then the goat's cheese, then the flaked trout and finally sprinkle the walnuts on top.

TROUT CAKES

When I make these trout cakes I usually do all the prep the night before and stick them in the fridge overnight. This means that when it comes to making dinner there is very little work to do. Fab for busy midweek nights.

....

Serves 4

2 tbsp butter

1 onion, diced

300g cooked trout, flaked

60g fresh breadcrumbs

2 eggs, beaten

½ tsp chopped parsley

1 tsp chopped chives

1 tbsp chopped tarragon

1 tsp salt

1 tbsp mustard

2 tbsp mayonnaise

2 tsp Worcestershire sauce

Oil, for frying

Melt the butter in a pan over a medium heat and fry the onion for 3–4 minutes until softened but not coloured. Remove from the heat and let cool.

Add all the ingredients into a large bowl and mix well – use your hands. Shape the mix into patties – you can make them whatever size you like. Lay on a plate and put in the fridge for 30 minutes.

Heat the oil in a frying pan over a high heat and fry the patties, in batches, for around 5 minutes each side until golden brown. If they are cooking too fast, reduce the heat.

feelin' fancy?

Serve with baby new potatoes and a crisp salad.

VEG

CAULIFLOWER 140

When cauliflower is in season you can find some huge ones to buy. They're usually called extra-large cauliflowers and cost between £1 and £1.50. This is what these recipes are based on, but don't worry if you can't get hold of one, you can just buy two smaller ones. Use one for the whole roasted cauliflower and one for the korma. You may be surprised to see a recipe here that uses the cauliflower leaves and another just for the stem or stalk. I used to think it was such a waste to throw them away so I did some research and found out that they are edible, and once I tried a few recipes I discovered they are delicious too. Result!

WINTER SQUASH 148

Winter squash come in all sorts of shapes and sizes. I had no idea how many varieties were available until a couple of years ago! When they are in season the supermarkets tend to have a few different varieties, but it is pot luck. If you want a specific type, then a farm shop or keen gardener is your best bet. There are differences in the texture and taste of the different varieties, which will affect the taste of your dishes, but they all work in these recipes.

When they are not typically in season you can still get butternut squash in most shops and, of course, around Halloween you can buy pumpkins everywhere.

MARROW 156

Again, when they are in season you can get some huge marrows. Not so much in the supermarkets but directly from farmers or growers. In fact, if you know someone who is an avid home grower with a veggie patch or an allotment, they often have a surplus of marrows they'd be happy to see someone appreciate. If you live near allotments it's worth taking a walk down, as some have a box near the entrance where the growers put excess produce for people to either buy or just take.

If you cannot find a marrow but want to try these recipes, you can use courgette instead – as a marrow is just a courgette that has been left to grow larger!

AUBERGINE 164

Did you know that aubergines are technically a fruit? A berry, in fact! But I am not suggesting you put them in your fruit salad.

Aubergines have a mildly smoky flavour on their own but are excellent at soaking up the flavour of herbs and spices. As you can see from the recipes here, they are extremely adaptable. Look for one with a bright green stalk that feels really heavy. That is when they are at their best.

WHOLE ROASTED CAULIFLOWER

This recipe makes for a beautiful dinner with the cauliflower as a stunning centrepiece. The paprika gets absorbed into the cauliflower, turning it a beautiful red colour. And the best thing? It tastes as good as it looks!

·················
Serves 4

750g new potatoes

6 Chantenay carrots

1 tbsp smoked paprika

70g butter, softened

2 garlic cloves, minced

1 tbsp oil

½ extra-large or 1 medium cauliflower

Preheat the oven to 180°C/Fan 160°C/Gas 4.

Parboil the whole potatoes and whole carrots in a pan of boiling water until just tender, about 5 minutes. Drain.

Mix the paprika, butter, garlic and half the oil in a small bowl.

Remove the leaves and stalk from the cauliflower and save for the extra dishes. Put the half or whole cauliflower in a roasting tin and brush over the marinade. Place the carrots and potatoes around the cauliflower and brush with the remaining oil. Cover with foil and cook for 20–25 minutes, then remove the foil, baste with the juices and cook for 5 minutes more.

CAULIFLOWER & SPINACH STEM SOUP

This recipe is basically made from the bits of veg you usually throw away – I was going to call it 'free soup'! You will be surprised at how tasty and filling it is.

Serves 4

½ tsp butter

1 garlic clove, minced

1.5cm piece of fresh ginger, grated

10 spinach stems, thinly sliced

5 cauliflower stalks (from the base of the cauliflower), thinly sliced

2 spring onions, thinly sliced

1 celery stick, thinly sliced

2 coriander stems, thinly sliced

750ml water

1 tbsp cornflour

½ tsp red chilli flakes

½ tsp sugar

½ tsp each of salt and black pepper

Heat the butter in a large pan over a low heat. Once melted, fry the garlic and ginger gently for 2 minutes. Add all the veg and herbs and fry for 5–6 minutes until tender. Pour in the water and bring to the boil.

Mix the cornflour with a little water to form a thick paste and stir into the soup, stirring continuously until it comes back to the boil. Add the chilli flakes, sugar, salt and pepper. Reduce the heat and simmer for 10 minutes.

Taste and add more salt and pepper if required.

feelin' fancy?

Serve hot with crusty bread.

CAULIFLOWER KORMA

If you love a korma from the takeaway, you will love this one. It's quick and easy to throw together and very filling. I was recently told it was 'superb'!

....

Serves 4

1 tbsp oil

1 onion, diced

3 garlic cloves, minced

2.5cm piece of fresh ginger, grated

1 red chilli, deseeded and finely chopped

2 tsp garam masala

1 tsp turmeric

100g ground almonds

1 x 400g tin chopped tomatoes

400ml vegetable stock

½ extra-large cauliflower or 1 medium cauliflower, broken into florets

200ml double cream

Handful of coriander leaves, to garnish

Heat the oil in a large saucepan over a low heat and cook the onion for 10 minutes. Stir in the garlic, ginger and chilli and cook for 1 minute. Stir in the garam masala, turmeric and ground almonds. Pour in the chopped tomatoes and stock, stir, bring to the boil, then add the cauliflower florets and simmer for 15 minutes until the cauliflower is tender.

Stir through the double cream and heat through. Serve the korma garnished with coriander leaves and alongside some rice.

CAULIFLOWER LEAVES STIR-FRY

After you have tried this recipe you will think back with regret to all the times
you threw your cauliflower leaves in the bin. This dish looks so
pretty and colourful and tastes great.

....

Serves 4

150g dried noodles

2 tbsp butter

The outer leaves from
1 cauliflower, stems
removed, finely
chopped

1 onion, diced

4 carrots, diced

4 celery sticks, diced

2 garlic cloves, minced

2.5cm piece of fresh
ginger, grated

1 tbsp soy sauce

½ tsp each of salt and
black pepper

Cook the noodles in a large pan of boiling salted water
until soft, following the instructions on the packet. Drain.

Heat the butter in a large frying pan or wok over a high
heat, and fry the cauliflower leaves for 2 minutes. Then
add the onion, carrots and celery and fry for 2 more
minutes. Add the garlic and ginger and fry for 30 seconds,
then add the soy sauce, salt and pepper and stir well.

Add the drained noodles to the wok and stir until well
combined. Serve immediately.

WINTER SQUASH GRATIN

I developed this recipe recently and it is absolutely gorgeous. I have made it numerous times now and every time it has been very well received.

....

Serves 4

700g winter squash

2 tbsp oil

1 onion, diced

1 garlic clove, minced

2 tbsp finely chopped parsley

1 tsp finely chopped sage

1 tsp each of salt and black pepper

3 eggs

120ml milk

60g Gruyère cheese, grated

30g Parmesan cheese, grated

Preheat the oven to 220°C/Fan 200°C/Gas 7.

Cut the squash into largish chunks and brush with 1 tablespoon of the oil. Lay on a baking tray and cook for 30 minutes.

Once cooked, separate the flesh from the skin and mash the flesh with a fork.

Turn the oven down to 180°C/Fan 160°C/Gas 4.

Heat the remaining oil in a large frying pan over a medium heat and cook the onion for 5 minutes. Add the garlic and cook for 30 seconds, then stir in the parsley, sage and squash and remove from the heat. Season with the salt and pepper.

Beat the eggs in a large bowl with the milk, then stir in the veg mixture and the Gruyère cheese. Put into a greased pie dish and sprinkle with the Parmesan. Bake for 30 minutes until lightly browned and sizzling.

Serve hot or cold with a side salad.

SQUASH & CHILLI SOUP

I am a huge fan of this soup. You get a great mix of sweet and savoury with each spoonful. It is truly delicious.

....

Serves 4

800g squash flesh, cubed

1 onion, diced

2 carrots, grated

2 parsnips, grated

50g porridge oats

1 litre vegetable stock

2 garlic cloves, minced

1 tsp mixed herbs

½ tsp chilli flakes

¼ tsp paprika

⅛ tsp ground cinnamon

1 tsp each of salt and
   black pepper

1 tbsp mango chutney

4 tsp plain yoghurt, to
   serve

Add all the ingredients except the mango chutney to the slow cooker. Cook on low for 6 hours or high for 3 hours.

Use a stick blender or masher to make the mixture nice and smooth. Stir in the mango chutney.

Divide among 4 bowls, and top each with 1 teaspoon of yoghurt to serve.

SQUASH & BEAN BURRITOS

This is a fab vegetarian recipe that can be made vegan by swapping out the cheese. These are great for serving if you have people round. I have made them for gatherings before as they are just as good hot or cold!

....

Serves 4

1 tbsp oil

2½ tsp ground cumin

½ tsp cayenne pepper

400g squash, peeled and cubed

3 peppers, any colour, deseeded and sliced

1 x 400g tin black beans

1 x 400g tin chopped tomatoes

1 x 340g tin sweetcorn

200g mushrooms, diced small

8 small wraps

100g cheese, grated

Preheat the oven to 200°C/Fan 180°C/Gas 6.

Mix the oil with the cumin and cayenne. Place the squash on a baking tray and brush with half the oil mix. Cook for 20 minutes in the oven. After 20 minutes add the peppers, brush with the remaining oil mix and put back in the oven for 15 minutes.

Meanwhile, add the black beans, tomatoes, sweetcorn and the mushrooms to a pan and simmer gently for 10 minutes.

Take the squash and peppers out of the oven and add to the bean mixture. Stir thoroughly. Divide the mixture between the wraps, fold the sides in and roll tightly.

Put the filled wraps in a baking tray and sprinkle over the cheese. Put under a medium grill for a few minutes until the cheese has melted and the wraps have crisped up.

Serve with a side salad or flavoured rice or couscous.

SQUASH PIE

Did you know that most 'pumpkin pie' in the UK is actually made with squash? This is mainly because we don't get pumpkin here throughout the year. If you make this once I guarantee you will make it again and again!

....

Serves 6

FOR THE PASTRY

200g plain flour, plus extra for dusting

¼ tsp salt

100g butter, softened

2 tbsp caster sugar

1 egg yolk

2 tbsp cold water

FOR THE FILLING

300g squash, sliced

1 tsp ground cinnamon

1 tsp ground ginger

¼ tsp grated nutmeg

25g soft brown sugar

2 tbsp golden syrup

170ml evaporated milk

2 eggs

Preheat the oven to 180°C/Fan 160°C/Gas 4.

Put the squash on a baking tray and roast for 30 minutes or until tender.

Meanwhile, make the pastry. Place the flour and salt in a large bowl and rub in the butter until it looks like breadcrumbs. Stir in the sugar, egg yolk and water and mix to a soft dough. Firm into a ball, wrap in cling film and chill in the fridge until the squash comes out the oven.

Roll out the pastry on a lightly floured work surface to line a 20cm round pie dish. Line the pastry case with a sheet of greaseproof paper and fill with baking beans and 'bake blind' for 10 minutes.

Meanwhile, mash or puree the cooked squash and mix with the spices, sugar and syrup. Stir in the evaporated milk and eggs and beat until smooth. Pour into the pastry case and bake for 25–30 minutes until the filling has set in the middle.

Allow to cool and serve with a scoop of ice cream.

SPANISH STUFFED MARROW

As well as tasting gorgeous, this dish looks gorgeous. I like to serve it on the table so everyone can appreciate how amazing it looks before tucking in!

....

Serves 4

2kg marrow

2 tbsp oil

¼ tsp each of salt and black pepper

200g chorizo, cut into chunks

1 onion, diced

1 chilli pepper, deseeded and diced

2 garlic cloves, minced

1 red pepper, deseeded and diced

1 orange pepper, deseeded and diced

½ aubergine, diced

1 tsp dried thyme

1 tsp dried oregano

½ tsp paprika

¼ tsp turmeric

150g rice

500ml vegetable stock

Preheat the oven to 180°C/Fan 160°C/Gas 4.

Cut the marrow in half lengthways and put half aside. Scrape the seeds from the other half, and use a spoon to scrape out some of the flesh – you want to get 300g to use in another recipe. Set aside. Place the scooped-out marrow on a baking tray and drizzle with half the oil and season with the salt and pepper. Roast for 1 hour.

Heat the remaining oil in a large pan over a medium heat and cook the chorizo for around 10 minutes, stirring occasionally, until starting to go crispy. Add the onion and chilli pepper and cook for 5 minutes. Add the garlic and cook for 1 minute, then stir through the rest of the veg, herbs and spices and the rice. Pour in three-quarters of the stock, cover with a lid and simmer gently. After 15 minutes, check and see if the rice is soft; if not, stir in the rest of the stock and cook for a couple more minutes.

Spoon the filling into the cavity in the marrow, then return to the oven and cook for another 20 minutes.

 feelin' fancy?   *Serve with a side salad and crusty bread.*

COCONUT MARROW SOUP

Oh yes! Who says soup has to be boring? This is soup-erb!
OK, no more jokes, I'll stick to the recipes!

Serves 4

2 tbsp oil

2 onions, diced

2 potatoes, peeled and diced

2 carrots, sliced

¼ extra-large marrow, diced

2 tbsp curry powder

500ml vegetable stock

50g creamed coconut

½ tsp each of salt and black pepper

200ml single cream, to serve

4 tbsp chopped chives, to garnish

Heat the oil in a large pan over a medium heat and fry the onions for around 5 minutes until softened but not coloured. Add the potatoes, carrots and marrow and fry for another 5 minutes. Sprinkle the curry powder over the veg and stir until coated. Pour in the stock, turn up the heat and bring to the boil, then reduce the heat to a steady simmer. Crumble in the creamed coconut and simmer for 15 minutes.

Blitz with a hand blender, then season with the salt and pepper.

Divide into bowls, drizzle with the cream and sprinkle on the chives.

ROAST MARROW SALAD

In summer I like to eat salad but it can get boring sometimes, so don't be scared to try something different. This will blow your socks off!

....

Serves 4

1 tbsp oil

1 garlic clove, minced

1 tbsp maple syrup

½ tsp each of salt and pepper

¼ extra-large marrow, sliced and each slice cut in half

2 tbsp hazelnuts, pecans or walnuts

2 slices of bread, toasted and blitzed to make crumbs

200g cavolo nero, stalks removed and leaves shredded

10 radishes, topped, tailed and quartered

100g Parmesan cheese, grated

FOR THE DRESSING

2 tbsp red wine vinegar

1 tbsp lemon juice

3 tbsp olive oil

1 shallot (or ½ small onion), diced

1 tsp mustard

¼ tsp sugar

Preheat the oven to 220°C/Fan 200°C/Gas 7.

Combine the oil, garlic, maple syrup and salt and pepper. Put the marrow on a baking tray and brush on the mixture, then cook for 20 minutes.

Sprinkle the nuts and breadcrumbs over the marrow slices and then cook for another 10 minutes.

Put the cavolo nero into a large bowl and add the radishes. Combine the dressing ingredients in a small bowl and pour over the cavolo nero and radishes. Use your hands to mix the dressing through the salad, massaging it into the cavolo nero.

Split the mix among 4 bowls and top with the marrow slices, breadcrumbs and nuts. Sprinkle some Parmesan on top before serving.

MARROW CAKE

Wait! What? Yes, cake! Real cake! I dare you to try it. Don't tell
anyone what is in it and see if they can guess.

....

Serves 16

150g butter

100g soft brown sugar

1 tsp vanilla essence

2 tbsp cocoa powder

250g self-raising flour

1 tsp baking powder

2 large eggs

2 tbsp milk

200g grated marrow flesh

FOR THE ICING

250g cream cheese

50g butter, softened

4 tbsp maple syrup

Preheat the oven to 180°C/Fan 160°C/Gas 4. Grease a
900g loaf tin.

Cream together the butter and sugar in a large bowl, then
mix in the vanilla essence and cocoa powder.

In a medium bowl, combine the flour and baking powder.

Gradually add the eggs into the butter and sugar mix
along with 2 tablespoons of the flour mix until smooth and
well combined. Stir in the rest of the flour. Add the milk
and marrow and stir well.

Add the batter to the loaf tin and cook in the oven for 50
minutes, or until a skewer pushed into the middle of the
cake comes out clean. Remove from the oven and leave
to cool in the tin, then turn out onto a wire rack to cool
completely.

While the cake cools, mix the cream cheese, butter and
maple syrup for the icing and put in the fridge for 30
minutes. Spread the cooled mix over the top of the cake.

Sprinkle the cake with roughly chopped
pecans.

AUBERGINE & CHICKPEA TRAYBAKE

We used to try to have a meat-free meal once a week, but in the last few years we have been increasing that. This is one recipe that we eat frequently and the bonus is it isn't just vegetarian, it is vegan-friendly too.

....

Serves 4

600g aubergine, sliced

2 onions, quartered

600g cherry tomatoes, cut in half

1 yellow pepper, deseeded and cut into chunks

1 orange pepper, deseeded and cut into chunks

1 chilli pepper, sliced

5 garlic cloves, crushed

2 x 400g tins chickpeas, drained and rinsed

2 tbsp oil

2 tsp Italian herbs

2 tsp garlic powder

1 tsp each of salt and black pepper

Basil leaves, to serve

Preheat the oven to 200°C/Fan 180°C/Gas 6.

Add the aubergine, onions, tomatoes, peppers, chilli pepper, garlic cloves and chickpeas to a large roasting tray. Mix the oil with the herbs, garlic powder and salt and pepper and brush over the veg, stirring so everything is coated. Cook in the oven for 25–30 minutes.

Divide among 4 plates and sprinkle with basil leaves.

AUBERGINE & LENTIL BALTI

Packed full of delicious veg, this is another recipe that is vegan-friendly (depending on balti paste used) – but your meat-eaters won't be disappointed as it is so tasty.

....

Serves 4

200g baby leaf spinach

200g frozen cauliflower

200g frozen cabbage

150g balti paste

400g aubergine, roughly chopped

2 x 400g tins chopped tomatoes

450ml vegetable stock

150g red lentils

15g chopped coriander

Bring a large pan of water to the boil, add the spinach and cook for 2 minutes to wilt. Lift out of the pan with a slotted spoon and drain, then squeeze out the excess water and roughly chop.

Put all the frozen veg in the same pan of water and bring back to the boil. Cook for 2 minutes, then drain and leave to dry in a colander.

Rinse out the pan then put it back over a medium heat and add the balti paste. Allow to sizzle for a minute before adding the aubergine and frying for 10 minutes. Add the chopped tomatoes, stock and lentils and bring to the boil. Reduce the heat and simmer, stirring occasionally, for 10 minutes. If it is too dry, add a little water. Stir in the coriander, spinach, cauliflower and cabbage and simmer for another 5 minutes.

feelin' fancy?

Serve with rice, mango chutney and flatbreads.

VEGETABLE MOUSSAKA

This vegetarian version of the classic dish is lighter but just as delicious. The aroma of this recipe as it cooks usually draws the kids from their bedrooms before it is even ready to serve!

....

Serves 4

100g red lentils

400g aubergine, sliced

2 tbsp oil

2 tsp each of salt and black pepper

1 red onion, finely diced

1 orange pepper, deseeded and finely diced

1 yellow pepper, deseeded and finely diced

2 garlic cloves, minced

4 tbsp tomato puree

1 x 400g tin chopped tomatoes

1 tsp ground cinnamon

2 tbsp finely chopped parsley

125g Greek yoghurt

125g ricotta

3 eggs

2 tsp freshly grated nutmeg

50g Parmesan cheese, grated

Preheat the oven to 180°C/Fan 160°C/Gas 4.

Cook the lentils following the packet instructions.

Toss the aubergine slices in the oil and 1 teaspoon each of salt and pepper. Heat a frying pan over a medium heat and fry the aubergine in batches for 2–3 minutes each side. Remove to a piece of kitchen paper to drain.

Add the onion, peppers and garlic to the pan and fry for 2–3 minutes, then stir in the tomato puree and cook for another 5 minutes. Add the chopped tomatoes and cinnamon and simmer for 5 minutes. Add the lentils and fried aubergines to the mix and stir well. Transfer the mix to a casserole dish and sprinkle over the parsley.

In a bowl, beat together the yoghurt, ricotta, eggs and nutmeg until smooth and well combined. Stir in the remaining 1 teaspoon each of salt and pepper. Pour the sauce over the veg and sprinkle on the Parmesan. Cook in the oven for 30 minutes.

feelin' fancy?

Serve with crusty bread.

AUBERGINE LASAGNE

This vegetarian take on lasagne is also suitable for people on carb-free diets. The pasta is replaced with large, thin slices of aubergine. You will be blown away with this!

....

Serves 4

1 large aubergine, sliced thinly lengthways

3 tbsp oil

2 tsp salt

½ tsp black pepper

450g mushrooms, diced very small

3 garlic cloves, minced

½ tsp dried oregano

1 tbsp tomato puree

2 x 400g tins chopped tomatoes, drained

1 tbsp Worcestershire sauce

400g ricotta cheese

50g Parmesan cheese

1 egg

300g spinach, finely chopped

250g mozzarella, shredded

2 tbsp chopped thyme

Preheat the oven to 200°C/Fan 180°C/Gas 6.

Arrange the aubergine slices flat in a single layer on a large baking tray. Brush them with 2 tablespoons of the oil and sprinkle with salt and pepper. Roast in the oven for 25 minutes, turning them over halfway through the cooking time.

Meanwhile, in a large frying pan, heat the remaining oil over a medium heat and fry the mushrooms for 7 minutes. Add the garlic and oregano and cook for another 2 minutes. Stir in the tomato puree, tinned tomatoes and Worcestershire sauce and bring to the boil. Reduce the heat and simmer gently for 15 minutes.

In a large bowl, beat the ricotta, half the Parmesan and the egg until well combined and smooth. Then stir in the spinach.

Take the aubergine out of the oven and reduce the temperature to 180°C/Fan 160°C/Gas 4.

Spoon half the mushroom sauce in an even layer in the base of a baking dish, then lay half the aubergine slices on top. Spread all of the ricotta mix on top, then layer the rest of the mushroom sauce over, then the rest of the aubergine. Top with the shredded mozzarella and remaining Parmesan and cook in the oven for 30 minutes.

Remove from the oven and sprinkle with the chopped thyme. Allow to rest for 10 minutes before serving.

LOVE YOUR LEFTOVERS

Personally, I love leftovers. To me, it means extra food I don't need to cook! But, for some people, I know it has negative connotations – they're thinking about dried up, reheated food that doesn't look or taste appetising. In fact, someone once said to me they didn't want to eat stuff that 'belonged in the bin' . . . I think they thought I was taking food that was left on people's plates and reusing it!

Don't worry, I wasn't!

And I wasn't because I never put too much on people's plates in the first place. When I used to have a little bit of something left, I would just put it out on plates with the rest as I thought there wasn't enough left to bother doing anything with it – I soon realised that extra bit usually ended up in the bin as it was just too much. So now I don't dish it up, I save it to be used in another meal.

As you will see from the recipes in this section, *nothing* goes to waste in my house. Apart from the money saving angle, I also think about reducing waste and helping to save the planet, so the recipes in this next section will help you feel good about both your wallet and your carbon footprint!

POTATO 174

RICE 180

PASTA 187

VEG 195

BREAD 202

FRUIT 210

POTATO

It is a well-known saying that if you have potatoes in the house you can make a meal. I love potatoes in all their forms, and I make my favourite potato items from leftovers – so much so, I often cook too many just so that I have some extra!

Even if I don't have a lot left there is always something to make with them. Boiled and roast potatoes are delicious fried in butter. Small amounts of mashed potatoes can be frozen in an ice cube tray and used to thicken soups and stews.

I often fill up my slow cooker with larger potatoes and 'bake' them. I can then wrap them well and freeze them for a speedy lunch or to accompany a meal. I also make my own frozen chips and roast potatoes by peeling, cutting and parboiling potatoes, then tossing them in oil and freezing them flat on a tray. Once frozen they can be bagged up to use as and when you need them.

I've included five recipes here for using up leftover potatoes, but I could have included a LOT more!

Oh, and btw, if you don't have leftover potatoes, you can use tinned potatoes in a lot of these recipes.

Pictured opposite: Bubble & squeak and Bombay potatoes

BOMBAY POTATOES

Another delicious way to eat potato. As if I need an excuse!

....
Serves 8

4 tbsp oil

½ tsp mustard seeds

2 pinches of chilli powder

½ tsp turmeric

¼ tsp salt

350g boiled potatoes, cubed

1 tsp chilli flakes

Heat the oil in a large frying pan over a medium heat. Add the mustard seeds, chilli powder, turmeric and salt. Fry for a couple of minutes to release the flavours.

Add the potatoes, stir well to coat in the spices and oil and fry for about 5 minutes.

Reduce the heat, sprinkle over the chilli flakes and cook for another 5 minutes until crisp and golden.

BUBBLE & SQUEAK

My favourite. I think this is the main reason I love Boxing Day. Bubble and squeak with cold meats and a poached egg. Bliss!

....
Serves 4

700g cooled mashed potatoes (rough amount – you can use more or less)

200g cooked cabbage or Brussels sprouts, or a mix of both, chopped

¼ tsp each of salt and black pepper

Flour, for dusting (optional)

2 tbsp butter

Mix together the potato and cabbage in a large mixing bowl. Season with the salt and pepper. If the mix is quite wet, add a little flour to stiffen it up, then shape into 4 patties.

Heat the butter in a large frying pan and fry the patties for 5–7 minutes on each side.

feelin' fancy? *I like to serve mine with a poached egg on top.*

POTATO SCONES

A Scottish delicacy that I often see people who have moved away pining after. I am
not sure that they realise how easy they are to make at home!

....

Serves 8

500g cold mashed
   potatoes

100g plain flour, plus
   extra for dusting

¼ tsp each of salt and
   black pepper

40g butter

*Pictured below: Potato
scones and Hidden veg
potato croquettes*

Put the cold mashed potatoes into a bowl with the flour
and seasoning and mix by hand to combine and make a
dough. Tip the dough onto a floured surface and divide
into 4. Roll the first lot of dough into a rough circle about
2cm thick, then cut into quarters. Repeat with each ball of
dough.

Heat the butter in a frying pan and fry each 'scone' for
2–3 minutes on each side.

These can be frozen for up to 3 months once cooked and
cooled, then grilled or fried to reheat.

HIDDEN VEG POTATO CROQUETTES

I've always loved potato croquettes, so when I found myself with some
leftover mash and veg I thought I'd try to make my own. Success!

....
Serves 4

250g leftover cooked root veg

500g mashed potatoes

Flour, for dusting (optional)

2 eggs, beaten

¼ tsp salt

Homemade breadcrumbs (a couple of rolls or slices of bread toasted and grated or blitzed in a food processor)

1 tbsp oil (if frying)

Preheat the oven to 200°C/Fan 180°C/Gas 6.

Mash or puree the leftover veg and mix into the mashed potatoes in a large mixing bowl. If the mix is a bit wet, stir in a little flour to stiffen it, then roll into 4 balls, croquette shapes or patties.

Place the beaten eggs and salt into one shallow bowl and the breadcrumbs in another shallow bowl. Dip the croquettes into the egg first and then the breadcrumbs.

To oven cook: lay the croquettes on a baking tray, evenly spaced, then cook in the oven for 30 minutes, turning halfway through the cooking time.

To fry: heat the oil in a large frying pan and fry for 8–10 minutes, until golden brown and crispy.

POTATO SALAD

My daughter LOVES potato salad. So I learnt to make my own – easy peasy!

. . . .

Serves 4

400g leftover cooked potatoes, cut into chunks

3 shallots, finely diced

2 celery sticks, finely diced

4 spring onions, sliced

3 tbsp mayonnaise

4 hard-boiled eggs, peeled and chopped

3 tbsp extra virgin olive oil

1 tbsp white wine vinegar

Small handful of parsley leaves, roughly chopped

Put the potatoes into a bowl with the shallots, celery and spring onions. Stir in the mayonnaise to evenly coat, then gently stir in the boiled eggs, without breaking them up too much.

Combine the olive oil and vinegar, then pour a little over the potato salad and keep tasting until you reach the required sharpness. Stir in the parsley and serve.

RICE

Rice is another thing that people usually make too much of and so it also often ends up in the bin. Folks tell you how dangerous it is to reheat rice and advise you not to do it, but in all honesty it is actually the cooling of the leftover rice that can be risky. You want to cool it as quickly as possible, because harmful bacteria can grow on it if it is kept warm for too long.

Some people run the rice under a cold tap to cool it but I found that method made it very tasteless, so instead I spread mine on a baking tray that I sit inside a larger baking tray full of icy cold water. The cold leftover rice can then be kept in the fridge or frozen – just make sure to reheat to piping hot before eating it.

Day-old rice is actually better for dishes like fried rice, which can turn to mush if you use just-cooked rice! Leftovers from flavoured rice dishes like jambalaya and risotto are perfect for making arancini, little deep-fried balls of rice and cheese or meat.

Japanese breakfast omelette 181

Buddha bowl 182

Rainbow fried rice 184

Cheesy rice cakes 185

Rice pudding 186

JAPANESE BREAKFAST OMELETTE

You have to try this. It may seem like a weird combo, but it just works!

....

Serves 4

400g any cooked rice dish – fried rice, jambalaya, biryani, etc

8 eggs, beaten

4 tbsp milk

4 tsp each of salt and black pepper

4 tsp oil

4 tsp butter

Microwave the rice on high for 4 minutes, stirring halfway through, and ensure it is piping hot.

Add the eggs, milk, salt and pepper to a large bowl and beat well, ensuring the whites and yolks are mixed properly.

Heat 1 teaspoon of the oil and 1 teaspoon of butter in a medium frying pan over a high heat. Pour in a quarter of the egg mixture – we are making 4 omelettes. Tilt the pan so that the egg covers the base of the pan. Once the base is cooked but the top is still slightly wet, add a quarter of the rice along the centre of the omelette. Now use a spatula to roll the edges up over the rice like you are rolling a burrito.

Carefully lift the omelette onto a plate and keep warm while you make the other 3 omelettes.

My kids love this for breakfast with tomato ketchup!

BUDDHA BOWL

Buddha bowls are a great way to get a balanced meal at lunchtime. You can easily change up the ingredients to suit your taste, your purse or whatever you have in the fridge. This is a good starting place if you haven't made your own bowls before.

....

Serves 4

200g salad leaves, torn

400g cooked and cooled rice

1 x 360g tin sweetcorn, drained

300g steamed beetroot, sliced

1 avocado, sliced

1 x 400g tin mixed beans, drained

100g salted peanuts

FOR THE DRESSING

½ cucumber, grated

350g Greek yoghurt

2 tbsp olive oil

2 tbsp chopped mint

1 tbsp lemon juice

1 garlic clove, minced

½ tsp salt

First make the dressing. Squeeze the liquid out of the grated cucumber and add the flesh to a bowl. Stir in the yoghurt, oil, mint, lemon juice, garlic and salt. Let the mixture rest while you assemble the bowls.

Divide the salad leaves among 4 bowls. Add the rice to the bowls then top with the sweetcorn, beetroot, avocado and beans in separate segments.

Sprinkle over the peanuts and drizzle the dressing over the Buddha bowls.

Pictured opposite: Japanese breakfast omelette, Buddha bowl and Rainbow fried rice

RAINBOW FRIED RICE

I love the look of this dish once it is cooked – a real rainbow on your plate.

....
Serves 4

1 tbsp oil

1 onion, diced

½ red pepper, deseeded
and diced

½ orange pepper,
deseeded and diced

250g frozen mixed veg
– a mix of carrot, peas,
sweetcorn, green beans
is ideal

2 garlic cloves, minced

1 tsp grated ginger

800g cooked and cooled
rice, preferably a day
old

4 tbsp soy sauce

2 spring onions, finely
sliced, to serve

In a large wok or frying pan, heat the oil over a medium–high heat, then add the onion and peppers and fry for 2–3 minutes. Stir in the frozen veg mix and cook for a further 2 minutes. Stir in the garlic and ginger and cook for 1 minute. Add the rice and soy sauce and stir for 2–3 minutes until the rice is piping hot.

Divide among 4 bowls and top with the spring onions.

CHEESY RICE CAKES

These are fab for lunches and snacks – super tasty and easy to make. My kids love them.

....
Serves 4

400g cooked and cooled
rice

2 eggs

2 tbsp breadcrumbs

50g Parmesan cheese,
grated

¼ tsp baking powder

50g parsley, finely
chopped

4 spring onions, finely
chopped

1 red pepper, deseeded
and finely chopped

1 tsp each of salt and
black pepper

Oil, for frying

In a large bowl, combine all the ingredients and stir well.

Heat 3–5cm of oil in a large frying pan over a medium heat. Using a large serving spoon, drop spoonfuls of the rice mix into the oil. Fry for 45 seconds each side or until golden brown. Cook in batches and don't crowd the pan. Transfer the cooked rice cakes to a plate lined with kitchen paper to drain.

Serve immediately with a dipping sauce of your choice – I like sweet chilli or BBQ sauce but the kids prefer ketchup.

RICE PUDDING

Unbelievably, I am the only one in my house that likes rice pudding! I know – shock horror! But it just means I can eat the whole lot. Not in one sitting, though – even that is too much for me. So I quite often have some for breakfast topped with some stewed fruit, or cold as a snack.

....

Serves 4

500ml milk

250g cooked rice, cooled

2 eggs

50g sugar

½ tsp vanilla essence

½ tsp ground cinnamon

50g raisins

Preheat the oven to 140°C/Fan 120°C/Gas 1.

Heat the milk and rice in a medium pan over a low heat, stirring frequently. Once boiling, reduce the heat to a gentle simmer.

In a separate bowl, beat the eggs, sugar and vanilla together. Whisk a ladleful of the hot milk into the egg mixture so it doesn't curdle when added to the pan. Add all the egg mixture into the pan, stirring constantly so the egg doesn't scramble. Cook until thick enough to coat the back of a spoon. Add the cinnamon and raisins and stir through.

Pour the whole lot into a casserole dish and cook for 30 minutes.

Allow to cool slightly before serving.

PASTA

Many, many people struggle with making the correct amount of pasta, and if you do too, don't worry about it. A couple of simple tips and a few recipes will make sure the excess doesn't go to waste.

But what to do with leftover cooked pasta? Most people think it cannot be reused, as once cooked it dries up and sticks together. I used to have a friend who would put the cooked pasta in water to stop this, but then the pasta kept absorbing the water and ended up a horrific sloppy mess. The trick is to add some oil and stir it through. You don't need a lot, but you do need to make sure it is well distributed throughout. Then you can go off and enjoy your meal before having to worry about what to do with your leftovers.

However, if you have leftover pasta that is already in a sauce, don't worry, I have some fab recipes to change that up too!

FRIED PASTA

Why had I never had this or even known it was a thing? I was intrigued when I heard that this is how leftover pasta is often eaten in Italy. Every day is a school day!

You need to have left the pasta in the fridge for this – preferably overnight – so that it has absorbed the flavours of the sauce.

....
Serves 4

4 tbsp olive oil

600g leftover pasta in a sauce

Heat 2 tablespoons of the oil in a large frying pan over a high heat. Once hot, add half the pasta and toss it around to get it all coated in the oil. How long to cook it for depends on how crispy you want it – I tend to do 8 minutes and stir every couple of minutes to get it evenly crispy. Remove from the pan and repeat the process with the rest of the oil and pasta – the pasta won't crisp up if the pan is too crowded.

 Serve with steamed mixed veg or a side salad.

Pictured opposite: Ham & greens pasta and Fried pasta

HAM & GREENS PASTA

This is also a good recipe to use up any leftover gammon.

....

Serves 4

500g spring greens, stripped from the thick stems and coarsely chopped

2 tsp oil

1 onion, diced

2 garlic cloves, minced

$\frac{1}{8}$ tsp cayenne

200g ham, sliced thin and cut into cubes

2 x 400g tins chopped tomatoes

600g cooked pasta

50g Parmesan cheese, grated

Bring a pan of salted water to the boil, then add the spring greens and cook for 10 minutes. Drain, rinse with cold water and press out any extra water.

Add the oil to a large pan and fry the onion for 3–5 minutes, then add the garlic and cayenne and stir for 30–60 seconds. Tip in the ham and tomatoes, mash down the tomatoes and simmer over a low heat for 20 minutes.

Add the pasta and spring greens to the tomato sauce, and stir through to heat and let the pasta absorb the flavours for 2 minutes.

Divide the pasta among 4 bowls and top with the grated cheese.

SPAGHETTI FRITTERS

I often make these for breakfast or lunch the day after I have inevitably made too much spaghetti! Tell me it's not just me? But to be honest I love these so much I have now started doing this on purpose.

....

Serves 4

400g cooked spaghetti in sauce

2 eggs, beaten

125g dried breadcrumbs

100g Parmesan cheese, grated

1 tsp each of salt and black pepper

2 tbsp olive oil

Roughly chop the spaghetti – I use scissors – and put in a large bowl. Add the eggs, breadcrumbs and cheese and stir to combine. Season with the salt and pepper and stir again. Try rolling the mix into a ball and check it holds its shape – if not, add a few more breadcrumbs until it reaches the desired consistency.

Heat the oil in a large frying pan over a high heat until very hot. Shape the mix into fritters – about 10cm in diameter and 5cm deep. Fry as many as you can fit in the pan without overcrowding them, cooking for 2 minutes, then flip over and cook for 1–1½ minutes until golden brown and crispy. Transfer to a plate lined with kitchen paper to drain while you cook the next batch.

feelin' fancy?

I love these served with a poached egg and asparagus. The kids prefer them with egg and baked beans.

PASTA & VEGETABLE PIE

My daughter gave me grief and said this isn't a pie as there is no pastry, but I just wasn't sure how I felt about calling it an omelette, so a pie it is. When she writes a book she can call her recipes whatever she wants!

....

Serves 4

600g cooked pasta

2 tbsp chopped oregano

400g frozen mixed veg, defrosted

¼ tsp each of salt and black pepper

4 eggs

185ml milk

200g cheese, grated

Preheat the oven to 200°C/Fan 180°C/Gas 6.

In a large bowl, mix the cooked pasta with the oregano, mixed veg and salt and pepper.

Whisk together the eggs and milk in a bowl and stir in the cheese. Pour over the pasta mix and put the whole lot in a pie dish. Cook for 20 minutes in the oven then cover and cook for a further 5 minutes.

Leave to cool for 10 minutes before serving.

PASTA & CHICKPEA SOUP

Did someone say taste sensation? Yeah, me! You will wonder why you have never had this before . . .

....

Serves 4

3 tbsp olive oil

3 sprigs of rosemary, finely chopped

2 celery sticks, chopped

1 carrot, chopped

1 onion, chopped

150g cherry tomatoes, halved

1 litre vegetable stock

1 x 400g tin chickpeas, drained and rinsed

200g cooked pasta or spaghetti

2 tsp each of salt and black pepper

2 tbsp parsley, finely chopped

50g Parmesan cheese, grated

Heat the oil in a large pan over a medium heat, and cook the rosemary, celery, carrot, onion and tomatoes for 10 minutes. Add the stock and chickpeas and simmer for 5 minutes.

Remove half the chickpeas to a bowl and roughly mash them with a fork, then return them to the pan. Stir in the cooked pasta and allow to heat through for 2–3 minutes. Season with the salt and pepper to taste.

Divide among 4 bowls and top with the parsley and grated Parmesan.

VEG

In my experience leftover veg is the food item most likely to get thrown away. People look at a spoonful of carrots or peas and think 'Not much I can do with that', but there is LOTS you can do with it, if you think outside the box.

The easiest thing – and perfect if you have fussy children – is simply to purée them and add them to sauces or gravy. And of course you can make them into a soup, too.

Also, it's worth remembering to save the vegetable peelings. Believe it or not, you can make amazing crisps from peelings! If you don't fancy that, you can put them in a bag in the freezer and once you have a lot, use them to make vegetable stock.

You can also regrow some veg, like spring onions and lettuce, by sitting the root in some water. Waste not want not, as my nana used to say!

ROOT VEG CRISPS

I am a fairly lazy cook so a lot of the time I don't peel my root veg, but when I do I never throw the peel away. Try to put these in the oven when it is on for something else. These crisps are fab and basically FREE! Can't get much cheaper than that.

....

Serves 4

3 tbsp oil

2 tsp ground cumin

2 tsp garlic powder

2 tsp paprika

1 tsp each of salt and black pepper

400g well-washed root vegetable peel – sweet potato, carrot, parsnip, swede, beetroot

Preheat the oven to 200°C/Fan 180°C/Gas 6.

Combine the oil, spices and salt and pepper in a small bowl and stir well.

Dry the veg peelings with kitchen paper, then put into a large bowl and add the oil mix. Stir well, making sure everything is evenly coated with the spiced oil. Put the peelings on a single layer on a large baking tray – you may need two – do not overcrowd them. Cook in the oven for 20–25 minutes, turning halfway through. Keep an eye on them as they may cook faster depending on their size.

Leave them to cool and go crispy, then enjoy as a snack on their own or with a dip, or sprinkle them over a salad.

Pictured opposite: Root veg crisps and Vegetable pakora

LEFTOVER VEGETABLE FRITTATA

I often cook extra veg just so I can make this frittata as it is so delicious!

·················
Serves 4

6 eggs

1 tbsp chopped parsley

1 tbsp chopped basil

2 tbsp butter

1 garlic clove, minced

400g cooked veg
(asparagus, sprouts,
cabbage, leek are best)

200g mozzarella

Preheat the grill.

Beat the eggs and chopped herbs together in a bowl.

Melt the butter in a medium frying pan over a low heat. Fry the garlic for 1 minute. Add the cooked vegetables and stir to coat in the garlic butter. Pour the eggs over the vegetables and stir through to ensure the veg is evenly distributed. Allow the frittata to cook for 10 minutes.

Tear up the mozzarella and scatter over the frittata. Put the frittata under the grill for 5 minutes or until the top has set and gone golden brown.

Leave to sit for 5 minutes before slicing and serving.

VEGETABLE PAKORA

No need to get on the phone to the takeaway if you fancy a wee treat.
This veg pakora is just as good – and a lot cheaper!

....

Serves 4

400g cooked veg
  (cauliflower, broccoli,
  sprouts, peas all work
  well – a mix is perfect),
  finely diced

100g green beans,
  chopped

1 courgette, grated

1 red onion, finely diced

100g spinach, shredded

1 green chilli, finely diced

50g coriander, shredded

1 tsp chilli powder

1 tsp ground cumin

½ tsp ground coriander

1 tsp tandoori masala
  powder

1 tsp each of salt and
  black pepper

200ml cold water

300g chickpea flour

Oil, for frying

Put all the prepared veg and herbs into a large bowl, and add all the spices and the salt and pepper. Pour the water into the bowl, then get your hands in and mix it all through. Gradually start adding the flour while still stirring with your hands – you are aiming to get a sticky mixture that is like a paste.

Heat the oil in a large wok or pan over a high heat – you need a good 15cm of oil. Once the oil is hot, drop in a little bit of the mix to make sure it is hot enough – it should start to bubble as soon as it hits the oil.

Start rolling the mix into balls about 5cm in diameter and drop them into the hot oil – carefully! Do not overcrowd the pan and cook in batches until golden brown. Remove and transfer to a plate lined with a piece of kitchen paper to drain. Repeat until you have cooked them all.

feelin' fancy? *Serve with a yoghurt and mint dip.*

CURRIED VEGETABLE PIE

I have been perfecting this recipe for a long time now. Over the years I have used all sorts of cooked veg and most work great, but root veg is best!

....
Serves 4

200g rice

2 tbsp butter, melted, plus 1 tbsp

1 egg, beaten

75g Parmesan cheese, grated, divided

1 onion, diced

1 red chilli, deseeded and diced

2 tsp curry powder

¼ tsp turmeric

250g cooked veg (root veg and squash are best)

120ml soured cream

120ml milk

2 eggs, beaten (keep separate from the first egg above)

Preheat the oven to 180°C/Fan 160°C/Gas 4.

Cook the rice following the packet instructions, then drain and cool under cold water. Mix the rice with the melted butter, the one beaten egg and 25g of the Parmesan. Press the rice mixture over the base and up the sides of a greased 23cm pie dish.

Heat the 1 tablespoon of butter in a large pan and fry the onion, chilli, curry powder and turmeric for about 3 minutes. Add the cooked veg and stir thoroughly. Spoon the mix over the rice pie base.

Combine the soured cream, milk, the two beaten eggs and remaining Parmesan in a bowl. Pour this over the veg mix and cook for 40 minutes in the oven.

TOMATO PASTA SAUCE

This soup is naturally thick and creamy, with a complementary kick from the chillies. Ideal for autumn, when squash is available in abundance.

....

Serves 8

1 tbsp oil

2 onions, diced

2 garlic cloves, minced

2 x 400g tins chopped tomatoes

400g cooked veg (ANY veg work in this recipe)

2 tbsp tomato puree

1 tsp chilli powder

1 litre beef stock

1 tbsp Worcestershire sauce

½ tsp each of salt and black pepper

100g soft cheese or cream (optional)

Heat the oil in a large pan over a medium heat and cook the onions for 4 minutes. Add the garlic and fry for 2 more minutes, then add all the other ingredients (except the cream/cheese). Bring to the boil, then reduce to a simmer for 10 minutes.

Blitz with a hand blender or in a food processor. If you want a creamier sauce, stir in some soft cheese or cream and mix through.

Mix the sauce through cooked pasta to serve.

feelin' fancy?

You could also add some cooked meat.

BREAD

I daren't even look at the statistics around how many bread products get thrown away each year. I'm sure I'm not alone in struggling to get the balance right; I either leave it out too long and it goes stale or I forget to take it out of the freezer and have to toast it for a sandwich!

Don't worry if your bread has gone a bit stale – as long as it's not mouldy you can use it up in lots of different ways. Croutons and breadcrumbs are the easiest way to save it from the bin, but there are many more practical and exciting ways to do it as well.

If we are having pasta for dinner, instead of buying garlic bread I often use normal bread that's just past its best – I simply spread it with some homemade garlic butter and grill it.

I use pitta breads as pizza bases or top them with garlic and coriander and have them with curry. Slightly stale wraps are perfect for quesadillas, and bread rolls, burger buns and finger rolls are fab for toasted cheese sandwiches!

Pictured opposite: Savoury bread & butter pudding
and Old-fashioned bread pudding

SAVOURY BREAD & BUTTER PUDDING

I am pretty sure you will already have tasted sweet bread and butter pudding before, but this savoury version is completely different. I could, quite happily, eat this every day!

....

Serves 4

25g butter, softened

1 garlic clove, minced

4 thick slices day-old white bread

12 cherry tomatoes, sliced in half

4 spring onions, sliced

50g cooked ham, roughly chopped

3 eggs, beaten

250ml milk

¼ tsp each of salt and black pepper

50g cheese, grated

Preheat the oven to 180°C/Fan 160°C/Gas 4.

Mix the butter and garlic together and use a little of the mixture to grease a shallow 23cm baking dish or tin. Use the rest to butter the bread. Cut the bread into triangles and arrange them in the tin, slightly overlapping each other. Tuck the tomatoes, spring onions and ham around the bread.

Whisk the eggs and milk together in a jug and season with the salt and pepper. Pour over the bread, pushing the bread down into the liquid. Leave to stand for 5 minutes.

Sprinkle the cheese over the top and cook for 40 minutes in the oven until puffed up and golden.

OLD-FASHIONED BREAD PUDDING

Use some old bread and your baking cupboard staples to make this delicious pudding.
Serve warm with custard or cold as a cake. Great for lunch boxes!

....

Serves 4

200g day-old bread,
  brown or white, crusts
  removed

500ml milk

200g dried fruit

50g suet

50g brown sugar

1 egg, beaten

3 tbsp mixed spice

1 tbsp granulated sugar

Break the bread into small pieces and put them in a large bowl. Pour over the milk and leave for 30 minutes.

Preheat the oven to 180°C/Fan 160°C/Gas 4.

Stir the bread and milk mixture with a fork to break it all up, then add the fruit, suet, brown sugar, egg and spice to the bread and milk and mix thoroughly – get your hands in and squeeze it together.

Grease an 18cm square baking tin. Pour the mix into the tin and flatten the top. Bake in the oven for 1 hour, then take out of the oven and sprinkle the granulated sugar over. Leave to cool in the tin for 30 minutes before slicing and serving.

STRAWBERRY CHEESECAKE FRENCH TOAST

If you want a real treat breakfast, then this will satisfy! I have started making
this for special occasions and the kids love it. It tastes like a lot more
work goes into making it than actually does.

....

Serves 4

400g day-old bread

8 eggs

400ml milk

200ml whipping cream

1 tsp vanilla essence

200g cream cheese

90g icing sugar

200g strawberries, hulled
and sliced

Cut the bread into 2.5cm chunks.

In a large bowl, beat the eggs, milk, cream and vanilla
together. Add the bread and let sit for 15 minutes.

In a separate bowl, beat the cream cheese and icing sugar
together.

Add the strawberries to the bread mix and stir. Tip the
mix into the slow cooker and flatten down. Dollop the
cream cheese mix on top. Cook in the slow cooker on high
for 2 hours, then serve.

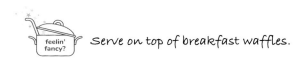
Serve on top of breakfast waffles.

BREAD SAUCE

Bread sauce doesn't have to just be for Christmas time. Use up any bread that
has gone a bit dry and you can treat yourself every week!

....

Serves 4

12 cloves

1 onion, quartered

300ml milk

2 bay leaves

6 peppercorns

100g grated day-old
  bread

75ml double cream

25g butter

¼ tsp each of salt and
  black pepper

1 tbsp freshly grated
  nutmeg

Push the cloves into the onion quarters, then put the
onions, milk, bay leaves and peppercorns into a pan, bring
to a gentle boil, then simmer for 5 minutes. Take off the
heat and leave to infuse for 30 minutes.

Strain the milk into a jug, then pour into a clean pan over a
low heat. Add the breadcrumbs and bring to the boil, then
simmer for 5 minutes. Pour in the cream, add the butter
and stir well. Season with salt and pepper and sprinkle
with the grated nutmeg.

SWEET MONTE CRISTO SANDWICHES

I make these as a treat in our house. Everyone loves them. It's a little bit of work, but totally worth it!

....

Serves 4

500ml oil

8 slices day-old bread, crusts removed

2 tbsp butter

2 tbsp strawberry jam

2 tbsp chocolate spread

1 tsp ground cinnamon

FOR THE BATTER

125g self-raising flour

200g caster sugar

150ml milk

A splash of sparkling water

Make the batter by sifting the flour and sugar into a large mixing bowl. Whisk in the milk and enough sparkling water to make a batter the consistency of single cream.

Heat the oil in a large, deep frying pan.

Spread 4 slices of bread with butter, then spread 2 slices each with jam and chocolate spread. Press together to make 4 sandwiches. Cut into triangles.

Test the temperature of the oil by dropping in a crust – if it bubbles, it is hot enough.

Dip the sandwiches into the batter, shaking off any excess, and then carefully lower into the oil. You will have to do this in batches. Cook for a few minutes until the sandwiches are golden brown. Remove from the hot oil using a slotted spoon and transfer to a plate lined with kitchen paper, then sprinkle with the cinnamon.

Serve hot.

Pictured opposite: Strawberry cheesecake French toast and Sweet Monte Cristo sandwiches

FRUIT

Unfortunately, fruit can be a bit of a nightmare to keep fresh and appealing to eat. There are lots of tips on how to store it properly – things like separate bananas from the bunch and wrap the ends in foil, wash berries in vinegar and water to make them last a little longer in the fridge, store cut-up fruit with a piece of kitchen roll on top to absorb any excess juice and stop it going mouldy – but inevitably you often find yourself with a couple of pieces of fruit that have gone a bit soft and wrinkly and you don't know what to do with them. I can help with that!

Most fruit can be frozen and then used in smoothies, or you can make some delicious fresh smoothies. Use yoghurt or milk as the liquid and a little honey or syrup if it ends up a bit tart. You can also freeze these smoothies on their own or with some granola in ice-lolly moulds for healthier hot-weather treats.

APPLE & PEAR STRUDEL

You may notice the absence of any raisins in this strudel, and that is because I am
not a huge fan. I absolutely love this recipe, though, which is ideal for using up fruit
that is bruised or on its way out. Feel free to experiment with different fruits
at different times of the year when they are cheap and plentiful.

....

Serves 8

2 apples, peeled, cored
and sliced

2 pears, peeled, cored and
sliced

1 tbsp ground cinnamon

3 tbsp brown sugar

2 tbsp lemon juice

375g shop-bought puff
pastry

Flour, for dusting

1 egg, beaten

Preheat the oven to 180°C/Fan 160°C/Gas 4.

Put the apples, pears, cinnamon, sugar and lemon juice
in a medium pan over a low heat and stir well. Cover and
cook for about 20 minutes until the fruit is soft.

Roll out the pastry on a floured surface into a large
rectangle. Lay your fruit mix along the long edge, leaving
a 1cm border. Fold the pastry over the fruit, wet the edges
and pinch together to seal.

Brush the pastry with the beaten egg and then cut 5 slits
in the top of the pastry. Cook in the oven for 20 minutes
until golden brown.

Allow to cool slightly before slicing and serving.

feelin'
fancy?
Serve with a scoop of ice cream or some warm
custard.

POACHED PEARS

If you are having guests round, this dessert looks and tastes impressive.
But it is a lot easier to make than you would think.

....
Serves 4

4 pears

200ml apple juice

3 tbsp lemon juice

1 tbsp sugar

1 tsp cinnamon

1 tsp vanilla essence

Peel the pears but leave the stalks attached.

Put the apple juice, lemon juice, sugar, cinnamon and vanilla in a large pan over a medium heat and cook for a couple of minutes until the sugar has melted. Sit the pears bottom-side to the base in the pan, cover and cook for 15 minutes until the pear is soft and tender.

Using a slotted spoon, very carefully remove the pears and set aside. Increase the heat under the pan and cook the sauce until it becomes very sticky, around 3–4 minutes.

Put the pears into bowls and pour the sticky sauce over them. Chill until ready to eat.

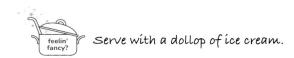

feelin' fancy?

Serve with a dollop of ice cream.

AVOCADO CHOCOLATE SPREAD

I can hear you exclaiming 'WHAT???', but I promise you this works.
And I promise it means you can get some healthy avocado into the kids,
whether or not they are aware what they're eating!

....

Serves 4

1 whole ripe (or overripe) avocado, peeled, pitted and mashed

25g cocoa powder

1 tsp vanilla essence

2 tbsp honey

¼ tsp salt

Add all the ingredients to a food processor or blender and blend until smooth. Taste to make sure it is sweet enough.

I love this served on toast or my banana pancakes.

It will keep for 2 days in a sealed jar in the fridge, but it never lasts that long in my house!

BANANA PANCAKES

I don't know anyone who doesn't like pancakes, and these banana ones won't be any different. I often make extra and lightly toast them to enjoy smothered with butter with a nice cuppa. Bliss!

Makes 12 pancakes to serve 4

1 egg

300ml milk

250g self-raising flour

2 bananas, mashed

1 tsp vanilla essence

2 tbsp butter

Beat the egg and milk together in a jug.

Sift the flour into a mixing bowl, make a well in the centre and stir in the milk and egg. Whisk until combined. Add the bananas and vanilla and stir well.

Heat a large non-stick frying pan over a medium heat, melt the butter and swirl it around to cover the whole base of the pan. Use a ladle to spoon in the batter to form little pancakes – don't overcrowd the pan. Cook for 2–3 minutes or until bubbles appear on the surface. Flip and cook for 2 minutes on the other side.

Transfer to a plate and cover loosely with foil until you have cooked the rest of the batches.

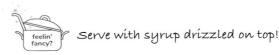 feelin' fancy? Serve with syrup drizzled on top!

Pictured opposite: Avocado chocolate spread and Banana pancakes

BERRY PUREE

I love fresh berries but they don't tend to keep very well. In summer when there are loads around you can often find them reduced in the supermarket at the end of the day. This recipe means that any going soft can be saved to be enjoyed at a later date.

....

Serves 20

600g berries – strawberry, raspberry, blueberry, blackberry or a mix (soft, overripe fruit is ideal for this)

80g icing sugar

1 tbsp lemon juice

Add the berries to a blender or mash with a fork. Stir in the icing sugar until it is dissolved. Add the lemon juice gradually to taste. Push through a sieve to remove the pips.

Keep in the fridge for 3 days or freeze in ice-cube trays and add to porridge, rice pudding, overnight oats or mix with plain yoghurt to make ice lollies.

BASICS

These are some basic sauce recipes that I think everyone should have.
They will help you cook the recipes in this book and hopefully give you the
confidence to experiment with cooking in general!

WHITE SAUCE

This basic white sauce, or béchamel, is the base for all creamy sauces,
such as cheese, parsley, peppercorn and mushroom.

....
Makes 500ml

30g butter
30g plain flour
500ml milk

Melt the butter in a pan over a medium heat, then stir
in the flour. It will clump together but don't worry – it's
supposed to! Cook for 2 minutes, then gradually stir in
the milk, whisking continuously until the sauce starts to
thicken and become smooth.

Depending on the end use of your sauce, add any extra
ingredients now, such as cheese, parsley, peppercorns,
etc.

Reduce the heat and simmer for 2 minutes to heat
through.

MINT SAUCE

A lot of recipes for mint sauce use white or red wine vinegar; I tend to use malt in mine as I prefer the flavour, but you can use whatever you have in. The best sugar to use here is caster, as it melts down well. If you don't have caster sugar, put whatever sugar you do have in a pestle and crush it or blitz it in a food processor for a minute.

....
Makes 500ml

30g mint, leaves stripped and torn up

250ml boiling water

2 tbsp malt vinegar

2 tsp caster sugar

Pinch of salt

Put the mint leaves in a heatproof bowl and cover with the boiling water. Leave for 5 minutes, then drain.

Meanwhile, mix together the vinegar, sugar and salt in a bowl.

Rinse the leaves with cold water, shake off any excess then add them to the bowl and mix well. Leave to infuse for 30 minutes before serving.

APPLE SAUCE

This recipe is a great addition to smoothies and overnight oats. It can also be added to porridge, rice pudding and lots of other savoury or sweet dishes.

....
Makes 150ml

50g butter

3 large apples, peeled, cored and sliced

3 tbsp sugar

Melt the butter in a small pan over a medium heat. Add the apple slices and the sugar and cook until softened, stirring occasionally. Mash to a pulp. Serve hot or cold, depending on your preference.

SALAD CREAM

I love salad cream! It is perfect for a quick salad dressing, divine on cheese salad sandwiches and so nice to dip proper deep-fried chips into.

....

Makes 200ml

2 hard-boiled egg yolks

2 tsp mustard

Juice of ½ lemon

3 tbsp white wine or cider vinegar

1 tbsp caster sugar

150ml double cream

Salt and black pepper, to taste

Milk, to thin

If you have a blender, add the egg yolks, mustard, lemon juice, vinegar and sugar and blitz until smooth. Add half the cream and pulse in short bursts, then add the rest of the cream gradually.

Taste and season with salt and pepper. If it is too thick you can add a little milk to loosen it to the desired consistency.

PERFECT MASHED POTATOES

I love mashed potatoes, but not the horrid lumpy ones I remember from school dinners! This is how I make mine.

....

Serves 4

500g potatoes, peeled and quartered

1 tsp salt, plus extra to taste

6 tbsp milk

120g butter, cubed

Black pepper, to taste

Put the potatoes in a large pan and cover with water. Add 1 teaspoon of salt and bring to the boil over a high heat. Reduce the heat, cover and cook for 15–20 minutes until the potatoes are soft but not watery. Drain them and set aside in the colander.

Put the milk and butter in the pan and heat gently until the butter is melted. Mix well and turn off the heat. Add the potatoes and mash well.

Once mashed whip with a wooden spoon and season to taste.

INDEX

THANK YOUS

My most sincere thanks must go to everyone who has thus far bought one of my books, or both previous books. I am not kidding when I say that without you, I wouldn't be in the very privileged position of being able to publish this third book. Thank you, thank you, thank you! And of course, I must thank the FYF Facebook community. You guys are my second family and I love you all so much. You make my days cheery and my job easy. I love the sense of community we all share so much.

Gaz and Sam, are you fed up with being thanked yet? No? Good, because I will keep thanking you for everything for as long as this crazy ride goes on. And Warrick, I said it in the last book, but I'm going to say it again . . . You are the MAN! Thank you for your sensible advice and for listening to my moans and freak outs.

To the Seaham crew, I love you guys – you are all just the right amount of mental! To G and Kate, good luck in your new ventures – I miss you already, but I know you are going to smash it. Just remember me when you are super successful businesswomen.

Carly Cook, you are a legend, and I will be forever grateful to you for helping me achieve this dream. Let's hope we can manage to get a drink and a catch up this time round.

To everyone at Orion, thank you for all your help and support. Anna Valentine – congratulations Mummy! Vicky Eribo, it has been a pleasure working with you. And Georgia Goodall, working with you again was fab. The magnificent Francesca Pearce, for all your hard work on book one and two and now three! You're always a delight to work with. To Nicole Abel for all your hard work, and of course to Clare Sivell and Helen Ewing for the top design work once again. Thank you to Helena Caldon and Rachel Malig for fixing all my silly mistakes.

To the amazing Ellie Mulligan for the fabulous cooking and styling. And, of course, to the one and only Andrew Hayes-Watkins – your pictures are stunning once again, and you're a top bloke. Thanks for making me so welcome at the shoot.

And finally, my family . . . John, I love you, thank you for everything. We are a top team! My babies – Ayla, Jamie and Kyle – you are my everything, I love you so much. Thank you for being exactly who you are, you make me so proud. To Paula, Alex, Morgan and Grace, I am so grateful to John for bringing you amazing young ladies into my life. You also make me very proud just to know you. And to my nephew Jordy, who demanded a mention in this book – you were a lovely wee boy and you have grown into such a lovely young man. If only you came over to visit your Auntie Lorna more often! I promise I'll make you some curry noodles or some lentil soup.

First published in Great Britain in 2022 by Seven Dials
an imprint of The Orion Publishing Group Ltd
Carmelite House, 50 Victoria Embankment
London EC4Y 0DZ

An Hachette UK Company

10 9 8 7 6 5 4 3 2 1

A CIP catalogue record for this book is
available from the British Library.

ISBN (Trade Paperback) 978 1 8418 8456 1
ISBN (eBook) 978 1 8418 8458 5

Publisher: Vicky Eribo
Editor: Georgia Goodall
Photography: Andrew Hayes-Watkins
Styling: Eleanor Mulligan
Design and Art Direction: Clare Sivell, Helen Ewing

Printed in Italy

www.orionbooks.co.uk